BILLBOARD
ART ON THE ROAD

A Retrospective Exhibition
Of Artists' Billboards
Of The Last 30 Years

Organized by:

Laura Steward Heon, Peggy Diggs, and Joseph Thompson

MASS MoCA
North Adams, Massachusetts
May – September 1999

BILLBOARD
Art on the Road

©1999 MASS MoCA
North Adams, Massachusetts
All rights reserved
ISBN 0-262-58177-9

MASS MoCA Publications
87 Marshall Street
North Adams, MA 01247
www.massmoca.org
Telephone: 413.664.4481
Fax: 413.663.8548

The MIT Press
Massachusetts Institute of Technology
Cambridge, Massachusetts 02142
http://mitpress.mit.edu

Contents

BILLBOARD

Acknowledgments

The authors would like to acknowledge the many people and organizations who were indispensable in the production of this catalogue. The support of several granting agencies and individuals was critical to the success of this project: the LEF Foundation, the Fund for Adams, the Artists' Resource Trust Fund of the Berkshire Taconic Community Foundation, The Outdoor Advertising Association of America, Margo Krupp, Berkshire Gas, Crowne Plaza Pittsfield-Berkshires, and Mick Callahan of Callahan Outdoor Advertising. Clark Art Institute slide librarians Libby Kieffer and Dustin Wees and readers' services librarian Nancy Spiegel provided critical assistance in the search for billboards. Finally, Meera Deean and Erin Curtis, MASS MoCA interns during the summer of 1998, were tenacious in their search for artists.

BILLBOARD

Foreword

Joseph Thompson
Director

The approach to North Adams, Massachusetts, by car is among the most exhilarating driving experiences in the United States. From the east, after a twisting descent down the Mohawk Trail and a riveting hairpin turn, Route 2 tunnels into town through industrial palisades formed by two massive red brick mill buildings rising sheer from the road's edge. From the south, Route 8 winds around Mount Greylock, the state's highest peak, through an eerily beautiful limestone mining operation. And from the west, leaving Williamstown, which actually calls itself 'The Village Beautiful,' Route 2 curls gracefully through the middle of Hillside Cemetery, arriving in North Adams at rooftop level before dropping into downtown. At every entrance to North Adams, one is slapped with the vital signs of raw commerce, industry, and trade: factory buildings, tightly packed worker housing, asphalt, steeples and smokestacks, and, most of all, billboards.

Zoned out of many Berkshire towns, billboards erupt in North Adams, providing color, information, and the feeling – in the midst of all the fastidious villages beautiful of Berkshire County – of a vivid commercial reality. I love the billboards of North Adams, not only for their designs, which are often stunning (and sometimes so odd and strangely anachronistic as to be surreal), but also for the way they set North Adams apart. There is something about the consciousness of this proud mill city that is reflected in the density of its signscape. Vivid, forcefully commercial, knit between the built environment and the lush mountains rising steeply from the downtown business district, the billboards are clinging survivors of an industrial past with a challenging, almost toxic energy.

When we opened the doors of MASS MoCA (sited in a once-abandoned mill complex that occupies one-third of North Adams' downtown), I wanted to extend the reach of the institution beyond our fence lines, and billboards offered a meaningful venue for that effort. Not only is North Adams a great billboard city, but with research it became clear that an important chapter in the history of art – artists' use of outdoor advertising media for public art projects – had gone mostly undocumented. The work deserved a comprehensive assessment: artists were not only utilizing the vernacular space of billboards, they were also appropriating the visual language and rhetoric of commercial advertising in their work and vice versa. The fluidity and richness of this interchange could only manifest itself in an exhibition of large scale. It also became clear that much of artists' work on billboards had been made possible by donations from the outdoor advertising industry – a substantial contribution to art, culture, and social communication that had gone largely unacknowledged. The marketing dividend that would accrue to MASS MoCA from 25 works of roadside art scattered across Western Massachusetts during our opening season did not escape us either. Joined by Peggy Diggs, an artist who has worked extensively in public art formats (including billboards), and by Laura Steward Heon (then a student at the Williams College Graduate Program in the History of Art at the Clark Art Institute, and now MASS MoCA's Associate Curator), I called Mick Callahan, who with his brother Dan are the fourth-generation owners of Callahan Outdoor Advertising. Mick gave an immediate thumbs-up to the project. With his endorsement, we received critical support from The Outdoor Advertising Association of America (OAAA) and other businesses that have helped finance *BILLBOARD* through sponsorships of individual billboards. The exhibition would not have taken place without these generous contributions, and we thank them all.

Finally, I join Laura and Peggy in expressing special gratitude to the artists who created new works for this exhibition (and the community members who collaborated with them), to the artists whose historic works are included in the retrospective, and to the other 87 artists whose work is documented here.

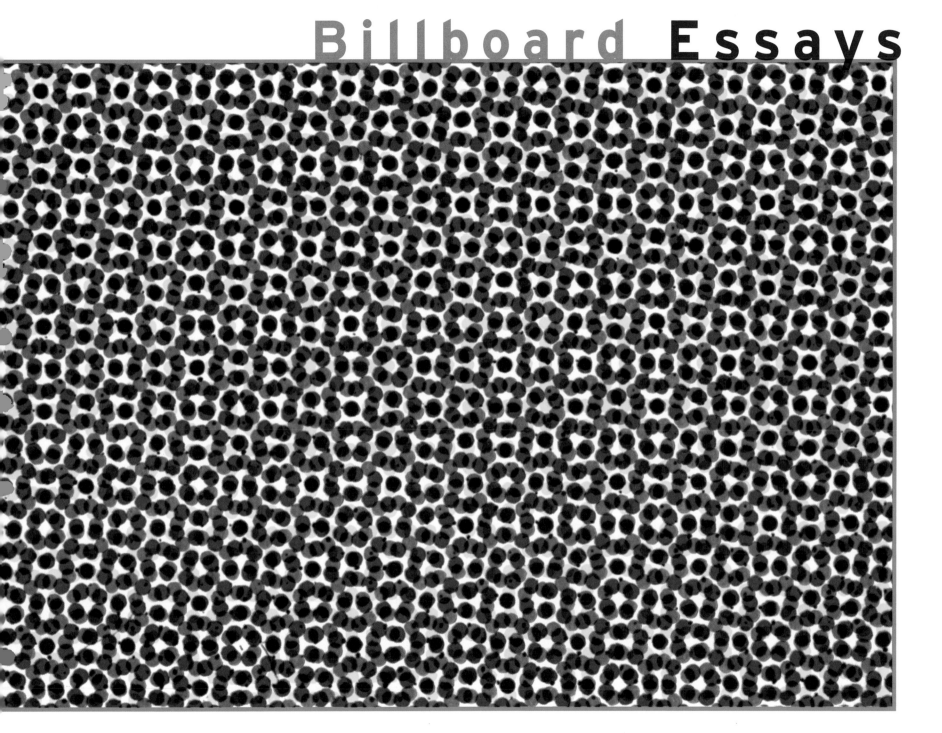

6

BILLBOARD

Putting
the Show
on the Road

Laura Steward Heon
Associate Curator

The term 'artist's billboard' has been used to describe everything from El Lissitzky's state-sponsored Constructivist admonition that *The Factory Benches Await You* to Gran Fury's spoof of a Benetton advertisement at the height of the HIV/AIDS epidemic, *Kissing Doesn't Kill, Greed and Indifference Do* (fig. 1). At its broadest, the term applies to any large poster mounted in a public place, whether for advertising, political propaganda, or even decoration. This diversity means there are many exhibitions of artists' billboards to be organized. It also means that, for the purposes of this exhibition, 'artist's billboard' has required a more focused definition.

FIG. 1 **Gran Fury:** *Kissing Doesn't Kill*, 1988

The objects in *BILLBOARD: Art on the Road* are works of art in the form of roadside billboards, bus billboards, bench billboards, and large bus shelter posters from roughly the last thirty years. Conceptual art billboards, social activist billboards, and billboards that are simply attractive images are represented. *BILLBOARD*'s catalogue features the works in the retrospective and those MASS MoCA commissioned, and also includes a wide-ranging survey of over two hundred and fifty additional billboards by artists.

The majority of the works included in the *BILLBOARD* exhibition and survey – and the majority of all billboards made by artists – address social issues that have held the attention of the artistic community at certain times. As Peggy Diggs argues in her essay, these billboards find cracks in the monolith of advertising and corporate culture in which to insert dissent. Often disguising themselves in the trappings of advertising, works such as Erika Rothenberg's *There Are Still Traditional Families* (page 66) are Trojan Horses, slipping into the built environment almost unnoticed, then springing their often radical messages on us.

FIG. 2 **Les Levine,** *Create Yourself*, 1987

FIG. 3 **Barbara Kruger,** *Untitled (Surveillance is Your Busy Work)*, 1985

The second largest group of billboards in the survey (but not the exhibition) includes charming, popular images by artists known primarily in their own communities, such as Mary Pratt's *Decked Mackerel* (page 64). The sizeable number of billboards made by artists with regional reputations, often with support of local arts councils or businesses, attests to the democratic, ecumenical appeal of billboards: they are readily available and affordable. For example, the Alabama State Council on the Arts, not known for considerable financial commitment to contemporary art, stands out for its numerous billboard commissions.

This accessible billboard space is obtained through rental or donation by a billboard company. An artist submits art (on a digital file, 4" x 5" color transparency, or camera-ready image) to the outdoor art advertising company, which then generates the billboard on paper or vinyl and installs it. Occasionally, the billboards may be hand-painted by the artist or the billboard company, but this practice is becoming supplanted by photomechanical and digital technologies.

A few artists, such as Les Levine (fig. 2) and Barbara Kruger (fig. 3), have made twenty or more billboards, though most artists have made only one or two. Motivations for making many billboards vary. Les Levine, for example, has made a long and successful career out of translating his sophisticated premises into billboards that have simple texts and images, yet are anything but simplistic. Often artists who have made numerous billboards, such as Levine, are committed to disrupting the flow of advertising from billboards to a passive audience by placing art in the path.

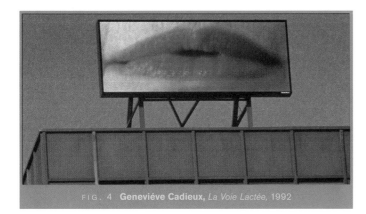

FIG. 4 **Geneviève Cadieux,** *La Voie Lactée,* 1992

A handful of billboards in the exhibition reflect an interest in the idea of communication per se, rather than a desire to communicate a particular idea. Geneviève Cadieux's *La Voie Lactée* (The Milky Way) (fig. 4), for example, gives no directive. A pair of lips, parted as if to speak, stretch across the billboard like its namesake, the Milky Way. The artist has placed a clear (if cosmic) reference to communication (the mouth) on an established site of communication (the billboard), resulting in a strangely mysterious work. Similarly, John Baldessari's *Man and Woman with Bridge* (page 50) combines abstruse, meaningful looks from a man and woman at opposite sides of an image (just what these looks mean, we do not know) with this obtuse form of communication, the billboard. These meta-communicative billboards, rich with unknowable meaning, have precedents in billboards made by Conceptualist artists Joseph Kosuth (page 61) and William Anastasi during the late 1960s. Such billboards are unusual because they do not draw from the two major precedents that Harriet Senie identifies in her essay, artistic advertisements and political propaganda.

As noted above, *BILLBOARD* includes bus billboards, bench billboards, bus shelter posters, and large subway station posters. These works are intended for the same audience as roadside billboards, must be understood in the same brief amount of

time, and require the same kinds of working procedures. The only real difference is in the scale and format. Alfredo Jaar (fig. 5), Barbara Kruger, Group Material, and Dennis Adams have all made billboards in these forms.

FIG. 5 **Alfredo Jaar,** *Rwanda,* 1994

Prankster, 'adbuster' or 'culture jammer' billboards, which appear in the survey but are not represented in the exhibition, are a phenomenon unlike any other in billboard art. They are usually witty graffiti interventions on standard advertising billboards, most often advertisements for cigarettes. The anonymous group Billboard Liberation Front has 'liberated' many billboards over the last twenty years, slyly altering them to subvert the original message, though without damage to the physical structure of the billboard site. The non-profit Media Foundation in Vancouver publishes *Adbuster*, a magazine featuring political interventions into advertising space, including billboards. The Foundation's mission is to "transform our commercial media culture and direct it towards ecological and social awareness."[1]

Its world wide web site provides a convenient diagram to make one's own "billboard buster," which is a simple tool that allows you to spray paint high above your head on a billboard. Culture jammers, such as the BLF and Ron English (fig. 6), share with other billboard makers a desire to disrupt the relentless delivery of commercial messages, though their methods differ drastically.

FIG. 6 **Ron English,** *Smooth Character,* 1994

The best artists' billboards are often place or time sensitive and address a specific audience. However, the very qualities that made them effective in their original contexts would render them out of place on the highways of Berkshire County. For example, a group of artists working in San Diego (Louis Hock, Elizabeth Sisco, and David Avalos) made an effective bus billboard (fig. 7) drawing attention to the use of grossly underpaid Mexican workers in the city's hospitality industry. Installed in San Diego during the 1992 Super Bowl, it altered the city's slogan, "America's Finest City," to "America's Finest Tourist Plantation" and included images of the workers. If this billboard were installed in this exhibition in the Berkshires, which has a thriving tourism industry, it would be interpreted as an irrelevant comment on this region, altering the original meaning significantly. Therefore, many such billboards are included in the survey, but not in the exhibition.

Instead, MASS MoCA commissioned five new works, which were made in consultation with residents of the region and installed near the Museum in North Adams and Adams, Massachusetts. These five billboards constitute the finale of the exhibition, since visitors driving to the Museum on the principal routes reach them last. Made by Lothar Baumgarten, Sue Coe, Gary Simmons, Julie Ault and Martin Beck, and Leon Golub, they introduce the Museum's regional community to its visitors during the inaugural season. The process for creating the five billboards grew out of MASS MoCA's desire for the new works to be community-specific. The artists were invited to North Adams for a weekend in October 1998 to meet with residents who shared their interests in topics as diverse as labor history, animal rights, and basketball. The residents were not there to tell the artists what they wanted on a billboard, nor were the artists to directly

FIG. 8 **Gary Simmons,** *Forever Champions,* 1999

represent the residents' feelings. Rather, the exhibition's organizers hoped that the artists would come away from this meeting with a sense of who the residents of the region are and how contemporary art might enrich their lives. Although some of the billboards clearly

reflect the exchange between artist and community – Gary Simmons's work (fig. 8) is an example – in others, the artists transformed a single idea that emerged from conversations (page 43). The five new billboards are presented on pages 37-46.

Billboards are ephemeral and almost always destroyed when taken down – so records of many of them are sparse, a fact revealed in the survey. The now defunct Eyes and Ears Foundation of San Francisco, for example, was a prolific maker and exhibiter of billboards, often churning out one every few weeks and placing it on the roof of its building at the corner of Eighth and Folsom Streets. The Foundation was responsible for over 100 billboards, the largest number by any single group, none of which are included in the survey because records are not available. The Revolution Gallery in suburban Detroit, by contrast, has ample information and photographs of the billboards that artists continue to install on the side of its building (fig. 9), and these works are well represented in the survey.

FIG. 9 **Culture Industries,** *Seditious Sound Bite,* 1997

FIG. 9 **Culture Industries,** *Seditious Sound Bite,* 1997

The artists' billboards of the last thirty years are an anomaly in contemporary art, not so much because they attempt to address a wide general audience, but because they often succeed. In response to the need for quick comprehension in a cluttered built environment, a billboard demands economy of design from artists, forcing them to pare down their images to essential, comprehensible qualities. The works in this exhibition engage the unsuspecting passerby with ideas that are often complex and mysterious, but which are expressed with great visual clarity. The coupling of reductive images with expansive ideas that a billboard requires is its salient quality as an artist's medium, and is a hallmark of the billboards in this exhibition.

1. www.webslinger@adbusters.org/information/foundation.html

12

BILLBOARD

Disturbances in the Fields of Mammon:

Towards a History of Artists' Billboards[1]

Harriet Senie

It Should Happen to You[2]

In George Cukor's 1954 movie *It Should Happen to You*, Gladys Glover (played by Judy Holiday) realizes her dream of being someone by having

FIG. 1 **Columbia Pictures,** *It Should Happen To You,* film still, 1954. The Museum Of Modern Art / Film Stills Archive

her name painted large on a billboard at Columbus Circle in New York City (fig. 1). Suave Evan Adams III (Peter Lawford), wanting the space to sell his company's soap, tries to buy it from Gladys, but she bargains instead for six alternative billboard sites. Her name attracts attention, Gladys becomes something of a local celebrity, and the soap company, capitalizing on her popularity, launches an advertising campaign around her image. As the stakes climb to a national tour, the interplay between Lawford and Holiday becomes ever more potentially sexual. Within a quintessentially 1950s frame, the film captures perfectly the allure of the billboard: fame and seduction – all that advertising can sell.

The appeal of the billboard, however, is clearer than its definition. The same term may be used for a kiosk in Paris, a huge sign on the highway, a spectacolor extravaganza in Times Square, and an image covering a moving bus. Part of the history of outdoor advertising, billboards are often referred to as posters. Not an ephemeral aspect of visual culture on the road, posters are a recognizable collectible, often ensconced in museums or for sale in galleries and stores; they have a distinctly 'art' connotation.[3] Here I will use posters to refer to portable works on paper (in various sizes) and billboards for the larger overall structures which project these signs of commerce and art into our midst.[4]

There may be no more telling argument for site being content in public art than the thus far unwritten history of artists' billboards. Usurping the spaces of advertising, they challenge more than the distinctions between high and low, art and design, gallery/museum and commercial work.[5] They ask implicitly if artists are capable of communicating directly with a general public, if art today is able to create even temporary disturbances in the fields of mammon.

European Posters for Art and Commerce

In histories of outdoor advertising, the antecedents of billboards are traced back to cave paintings. Greek tablets posted schedules of public games; Roman signs pertained to politics as well as business. Carried on foot or pasted to walls, outdoor advertising expanded in tandem with advances in printing technology and the growth of cities and mass transportation.[6] By the end of the nineteenth century, posters were considered "an active medium for the selling of ideas, the motivation of consumers and the expression of artistic and design ideals."[7]

Greatly influenced by Japanese woodblock prints (often used for advertising Kabuki theater), Impressionist artists created posters for performances and products associated with the newly found leisure time of the middle class. Most famously, Henri de Toulouse-Lautrec's

posters featured contemporary cabaret entertainment (fig. 2). Recognized as art and advertising, Parisian posters affixed to kiosks and buildings, addressing strollers along the broad boulevards of the city, projected a way of life that came to define the bourgeois culture of the time.[8]

In early twentieth-century Europe, the modern poster of the Bauhaus in Germany, De Stijl in Holland, and Constructivism in Russia was associated with overtly utopian and political aims. With an emphasis on simple geometric shapes, "the idealists of the 1920s hoped to create a universal visual vocabulary … (that) was symbolic of ideas."[9] Trying to merge art and design (or eradicate their distinction), artists like Rodchenko, trying to encompass and define Russia's new political system, used posters to advertise the state airline, table oil, cookies, and cigarettes, as well as trade unions and films.[10] Artists of the modern poster in Europe built on traditions of art and advertising, addressing politics as well as products, sometimes as one and the same.

Billboards as Environmental Blight

"The battle against the billboard is almost as old as the billboard itself."
William H. Wilson, *The Billboard: Bane of the City Beautiful*

Praised by some as the art gallery of the man (sic) on the street and the highway, but more often damned as a visual plague that had to be contained, billboards were attacked (again and again) as environmental blight that was badly in need of civic control. By the end of the nineteenth century, posters in European cities such as Paris and Berlin were gradually confined to specially designed free-standing structures maintained by municipally franchised private companies.[11] In the United States anti-billboard campaigns emerged as part of the City Beautiful Movement, a turn-of-the-century reform effort mounted by professional architects and planners as well as citizen activists concerned with the degenerating conditions and appearance of the country's urban areas.[12] Indeed, there was cause for alarm. The building of railroads was accompanied by a proliferation of ever larger billboards deemed necessary to attract a faster moving eye. Commerce's apparent quest for the largest billboard, comparable to a later race for the tallest skyscraper, resulted in several astonishing examples. In 1897 Schlitz beer signs covered eight Chicago grain elevators; a billboard advertising Lea & Perrins Sauce erected two years later along the Erie Basin Breakwater facing New York Bay measured 16' x 2,360'.[13]

With Frederick Olmstead, Jr. among their more moderate detractors, billboards in cities and rural areas were attacked for obscuring natural vistas and constituting a visual affront. As a disproportionate number of billboards advertised whiskey, beer, and tobacco, part of the anti-billboard campaign in the United States became a moral issue of potential corruption of the young. Additional arguments focused on their nuisance value as obstructions concealing trash and nefarious activities, oddly prefiguring similar attacks that were leveled, more than half a century later, against large-scale public sculpture.[14]

In response, the billboard industry (much like the public art constituency later) argued the economic advantages of their product. Billboards generated revenues for property owners (who leased their space or buildings), lumber and hardware trades, and the printing and graphic design industries. Advocates also cited their products' "power to inform, instruct, amuse and divert."[15]

In the end, the battle was temporarily settled in the courts. Following the arguments of the City Beautiful reformers, billboards were recognized as "a separate class of structures requiring distinct regulations."[16] Once this was legally established and a precedent set, it became possible to continue the fight for control of the visual environment outside the museum.

Early American Modernism and the Romance of Commerce

"The bold, framed, and freestanding billboard is an American invention. Its scale fits the American landscape and conveys its advertising message directly."
James Fraser, *The American Billboard: 100 Years*

While many early twentieth century modernists were fascinated by the rapidly changing urban and rural environments of the United States, others were equally repelled.[17] It has even been suggested that development of art in the United States might well be considered in terms of its love/hate relationship with commercial and popular culture.[18] Seen from abroad, these were (and continue to be) the defining and most seductive aspects of the American way of life.

For many, billboards out there on the road connote not only the quintessential American ad, but "modernity American-style."[19] Several significant modern artists painted them and used their visual vocabulary to develop a style dubbed "billboard cubism" by art historian Wanda Corn.[20] Thus she suggests that Charles Demuth's 1928 *I Saw The Figure 5 in Gold* may be "read as a poster or billboard advertisement for William Carlos Williams, the Great Figure of American Poetry" an example of his search for "a new poetics based on the language of billboards and electric signs."[21]

The prosperous twenties were a boom time for outdoor advertising, and it was easy to associate the new product ads of the period with the youthful, carefree life identified with the jazz age. But the Great Depression that ended the decade signalled, at least for a time, that the romance was over. Photographers like Margaret Bourke-White and Walker Evans used billboards as points of ironic contrast between the lifestyle portrayed in the ads and the existence endured by millions of Americans.

Evans, whose father had worked in advertising (first as an agent for the Wabash Railroad and later as copywriter for Lord and Thomas in Chicago), had a lifelong fascination with signs.[22] He photographed them repeatedly, collected them, and sometimes even exhibited them together with his work. Even in apparently neutral images, such as a 1929 photograph of outdoor advertising in Times Square (fig. 3), Evans worked "in conscious opposition to whatever 'meaning' the signs themselves were intended to communicate."[23] Using cropping techniques that interrupted instantaneous recognition and revealing the processes behind the presentation, Walker prefigured the strategies of later artists who made billboards using or deconstructing traditional techniques of advertising in order to subvert them.

FIG. 3 **Walker Evans,** *Outdoor Advertisements,* gelatin silver print, c.1929. The J. Paul Getty Museum, Los Angeles.

Billboards for War

"The twentieth century busted out in a babble of words whose din was overcome briefly only by the loud explosions of World War I." Andrei Cordrescu

In 1912, in response to widespread negative campaigns and legislation, the Associated Billposters Association of the United States and Canada changed its name to the Poster Advertising Association to distance itself from the urban blight associated with the billposter. Among its public relations efforts, an education committee, established the following year, developed public service posters. These were presented as an industry responsibility, an opportunity to fill 'open beds' with messages ranging from the inspirational to safety concerns.[24]

World War I offered just such an opportunity. The day after the United States declared war on Germany on April 6, 1917, a meeting was called by the president of the Association of Advertising Clubs of the World and the Poster Advertising Association "to mobilize industry."[25] Among the best known World War I recruitment posters were James Montgomery Flagg's image of a pointing *Uncle Sam I Want You for the U.S. Army* and Joseph C. Leyendecker's *Get in the Game with Uncle Sam*, with Sam portrayed as a slugger holding a baseball bat at the ready. Equally aggressive images, such as John Scott Williams' *Liberty* as a sword-wielding, shield-bearing goddess of war, commanded citizens to buy war bonds. Some advertisers, linking their product to the war cause, not only managed to keep their brand names in the public eye but managed to make their consumption seem patriotic. (fig. 4) Overall, the industry's participation in the war effort, coupled with newly enacted legislation, appeared effective in stemming previous City Beautiful attacks against billboards.[26]

While it was estimated that the outdoor advertising industry gave more than $1.5 million to the war cause, the art community also rallied. George William Eggers, acting director of the Art Institute of Chicago, issued a "call to service," positing national service art against art for art's sake; the New York School of Fine and Applied Art had faculty and students alike making posters for the Army and National Guard, and art schools and universities gave courses on war poster art.[27] The figurative style of war posters in the United States, closely related to contemporary magazine illustrations, emphasized the preference for narrative over geometric abstraction and human interest over visual idea.[28]

Little changed during World War II except the focus of the propaganda. "Addressing every citizen as a combatant in a war of production," these posters were intended "to sell the idea that the factory and the home were also arenas of war."[29] Not surprisingly, the flag figured prominently, perhaps more so than Uncle Sam. The most popular poster design of the war, created by Carl Paulson for a United States Treasury Department bond campaign, was displayed as a billboard in

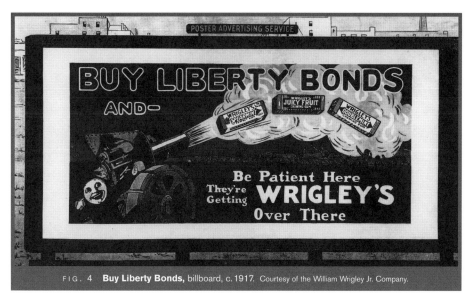

The government publicity campaign for the war effort, including billboards and posters, aimed at creating a broad base of national solidarity and support. Under a mantle of patriotism, the outdoor advertising industry helped create and proliferate images of national icons, wherever possible linking them to consumable products. War billboards and posters, the prime example of the public service billboard, established a precedent for subsequent artists' billboards that addressed political and social issues. They also created a visual environment that may have directly influenced the Pop artists of the next generation.

Advertising into Art: the Great American Pop Art Debates

With a renewed recognition that visual culture in the United States was largely defined by advertisements promoting the American way of capitalist consumption, Pop Art in the early sixties ushered the language and images of advertising into the museum on a large scale.[34] Different from earlier twentieth century celebrations of the new commercial and industrial American landscape such as Gerald Murphy's *Razor* (fig. 5) and Demuth's *My Egypt*, this generation of admen-turned-artists understood first-hand the advertising process behind the product and expressed a more obviously ambiguous attitude towards their subjects.

more than 30,000 locations across the country in March and April of 1942. Used again in subsequent billboard campaigns, it proved so popular that the Government Printing Office printed four million small color reproductions to meet public demand.[30]

For the most part smaller than billboards, and therefore not as closely linked to advertising, these posters were placed in unexpected places such as train stations, schools, restaurants, and retail stores. Initially eschewing the aggressive style of World War I posters, these images focused on participation and citizenship investment (and therefore ownership) of the national effort. Gradually the emphasis shifted from defense to victory.[31] Arguments over the most effective poster styles reflected different conceptions of the public, pitting advertising ideals against art world values, the latter advocating 'war graphics' over more directly emotional and realistic images. Regardless of style, however, the government wanted to portray the civilian participation in the war effort in a positive light, never suggesting the connection between bond money and bloody battlefields.[32]

While Demuth's titles held a tinge of irony, in his paintings he both recognized and admired the emerging industrial landscape. The Pop artists of the 1960s, however, were concerned with the cumulative effects of the array of commercial visual culture. Andy Warhol focused on the sameness of it all, Roy Lichtenstein on its sound byte visual and verbal simplicity, and James Rosenquist on an updated version of 'billboard cubism' that revealed how art might easily be used to obscure commercial content. Although there was a great allure in this early work of the 1960s, there was also an inherent dark side.

Warhol showed us that the packaging of people and art was no different from the packaging of products (Marilyn, Mona Lisa, soup); Lichtenstein focused on the stereotypical gender roles depicted in comics of love and war (*Engagement Ring* and *Whaam!*), and Rosenquist turned his fragmented focus to the actual fragmentation of the landscape (*F-111*).

While critics argued over whether or not this was the decline of art, a critique or a celebration of consumer culture, the public seemed to love it. It became – surprise! – instantly popular.[34] As the images of Pop Art taken from consumer-defined life proliferated, they were recycled into the culture that had inspired them as T-shirts, toys, and tchotchkes. The continuum that existed between the commercial world and Pop was perfectly recognized by a series of three exhibitions titled *Signs of the Times* that opened at the Des Moines Art Center in late 1963: *Trade Signs and Symbols of the Nineteenth Century, Poster and Billboard Art of the Nineteenth and Early Twentieth Centuries,* and *Work by Twelve Contemporary Pop Artists.* [35] While the exhibitions offered evidence of an ongoing fascination with what director Thomas S. Tibbs called the 'Trade Marks' of an era, Pop Art had, I believe, a more seditious soul.

What Pop artists managed to convey with their dead-pan Andy attitude was both the seduction of their images and the emptiness of the surface way of life they defined. They were able to capture and hold in perfect equilibrium the tension of irreconcilable opposites that so often defines the experience of contemporary life. At the same time they seem separate from their sources, somehow questioning the reality of it all.[36] But the strategies of Pop, calling on the viewer to decode the message, to decide what it meant or not, set the tone for the artists' billboards of the following decades that dared venture into the sites of advertising to challenge the pre-coded assumptions associated with them.[37]

FIG. 6 **Guerrilla Girls.** *Met. Museum,* billboard design, 1988. Courtesy of the Guerrilla Girls.

Off the Road (Again)

As with Pop Art, the architecture of the new commercial sprawl had its detractors and champions. Among the former, Peter Blake's 1964 *God's Own Junkyard: The Planned Deterioration of America's Landscape*, picking up the cry of the earlier City Beautiful movement critics, summed up the nay-sayers: "Our towns and cities boast many isolated handsome buildings – but very few handsome streets, squares, civic centers, or neighborhoods – our suburbs are interminable wastelands dotted with millions of monotonous little houses on monstrous little lots and crisscrossed by highways lined with billboards, jazzed-up diners, used-car lots, drive-in movies, beflagged gas stations, and garish motels."[38] Worried that the billboard lobbies offering free space to political candidates on influential committees would prevail, Blake pointed out that billboards caused accidents, and California Governor Pat Brown compared a billboard blocking a view to littering the highways with refuse.

Once again the environmental focus of the time prevailed, this time most famously supported by Lady Bird Johnson. The Great Society Task Force was created in 1964, the Department of Housing and Development was created in 1965, and a year later the Model Cities Act was passed.

While Washington passed legislation to limit the look of Las Vegas et al, Robert Venturi and crew, more in sync with the new Pop Art sensibility, visited that infamous city and liked what they found. In 1966 he published *Complexity and Contradiciton in Architecture*, signalling a major shift from the aesthetic of pristine modern architecture perhaps best exemplified by Mies van der Rohe.[39] Introduced by architectural historian Vincent Scully as the most important writing on architecture since Le Corbusier's *Vers une Architecture* of 1923, Venturi argued not only for complexity and contradiction, but also ambiguity, multiple readings, and the ironic convention. His *Learning from Las Vegas: The Forgotten Symbolism of Architectural Form* written with Denise Scott Brown and Steven Izenour and published five years later, was a logical outgrowth of his ironic embrace of the Main Street aesthetic. In a section entitled "Billboards are almost all right," they observed: "The Italian landscape has always harmonized the vulgar and the Vitruvian: the contorni around the duomo, the portiere's laundry across the padrone's portone, Supercortemaggiore against the Romanesque apse. Naked children have never played in our fountains, and I.M. Pei will never be happy on Route 66."[40]

Art in Place of Advertising: Subjects, Strategies, and Sites

"Art is a practice, and insofar as it makes consciousness, it participates in making the world." Joseph Kosuth

A post-pop generation of artists and critics worried less about the stigma of commerce than the growing socio-political ills of society. With the emergence of public art in the late 1960s and broad-based political protest surrounding the Vietnam War, the environment, civil rights, and feminism, artists increasingly addressed public issues, spaces, and audiences.[41] Artists' billboards flourished largely during the 1980s before arts funding had dwindled, in response to growing alarm over the social neglect of the Reagan and Bush administrations and the pervasive stupefying effects of the media.

At a time when public sculpture was increasingly criticized for failing to address public interests, overtly political art neutralized by a museum setting, and interactive community projects often denigrated as social work, artists' billboards provide a viable alternative. While some addressed general issues of ecology or prejudices pertaining to race, ethnicity, gender, and sexual preference, others

tried to alter attitudes towards AIDS. Attempting to effect change or challenge prevailing stereotypes, artists used billboards to address the major social issues of the day.[42]

Prompting thoughts rather than purchases, artists appropriated the techniques and spaces of advertising. They focused on awareness, citizen participation, and personal responsibility, just as earlier generations of public service billboards emphasized the war effort at home. Their mode of address varied depending on their intention, prodding, pleading, or (just) presenting the facts.

Creating Awareness

Just as earlier in the century women used posters to campaign for women's suffrage, the Guerrilla Girls addressed art world inequities.[43] In the tradition of feminist consciousness-raising of the 1970s, the Guerrilla Girls a decade later created posters and billboards revealing the damning statistics of prevalent museum and gallery sexist (and racist) practices.[44] In 1985 one poster asked *HOW MANY WOMEN HAD ONE-PERSON EXHIBITIONS AT NYC MUSEUMS LAST YEAR? (None at the Guggenheim, Metropolitan, and Whitney Museums; one at the Modern).* A few years later one queried *Do women have to be naked to get into the Met. Museum?*, which focused attention on the disparity between the museum's collection of work by women artists as opposed to their depictions of female nudes (less than 5% vs. 85%) (fig. 6).[45] A women's collaborative whose members wore gorilla masks for public performances and picket lines, the Guerrilla Girls attracted widespread media attention, giving form to suspicion, making people start paying attention to the numbers.

Inequities may also be revealed by recasting the powerful as powerless. (I have yet to see the reverse, although I imagine it might be equally effective.) Barbara Kruger's 1991 poster on reproductive rights and life choices reversed biological and socialized gender roles.[46] Appearing on 90 bus shelter billboards around New York City, three different images of men yell "HELP!" because, as the text below revealed, they are pregnant and stymied by choices they are now forced to make between personal and professional goals.[47]

Empowering

Giving a voice to the unheard and addressing those in need, artists' billboards offered visibility and help. *Your Message Here*, a 1990 billboard project in Chicago organized by the collaborative Group Material and others addressed issues ranging from respect for the homeless to respect for the neighborhood.[48] In an area where illegal immigration was a problem, one image stated *Ningún Humano Es Ilegal* (fig. 7). The forty billboards by inner-city community-based organizations and individuals changed location every three months to increase communication among diverse groups.[49]

FIG. 7 **Group Material and Randolph Street Gallery,** *Nigún Humano Es Ilegal,* billboard, 1990. Courtesy of the artists.

Empowerment may also consist of offering assistance. Kruger's 1992 San Francisco billboard of a disfigured face behind a chain link fence under the caption "*If you are beaten/If you are hurt/If you are scared/If you need help*" directed the viewer to "GET OUT" and offered a number to call (fig. 8). An earlier 1988 billboard by Stein Robaire Helm and Creston Communications for the Los Angeles Commission on Assaults Against Women used a horizontal image of a women in a body bag under the statement, "Some women will never talk to anyone about being abused." Both displayed the local telephone number of the National Domestic Violence Hotline.

FIG. 8 **Barbara Kruger,** *GET OUT,* bus shelter, 1992. Courtesy of Y-Core, Chicago and the Liz Claiborne Foundation.

FIG. 9 **G.H. Hovagimyan,** *Hey Bozo ... Use Mass Transit,* billboard, 1990. Courtesy of the artist.

Exhorting to Action

Ecology issues usually require a basic change in behavior (rather than a single phone call). In 1990 New York City's Metropolitan Transportation Authority (MTA) Arts for Transit working with Creative Time, an independent public art organization, began a five-year billboard campaign to get New Yorkers out of their cars and into mass transit.[50] The design that generated the greatest public response was G.H. Hovagimyan's *Hey Bozo* image of a doll in clown makeup driving a kiddie car next to a rap-type text on a fluorescent orange background, addressing the viewer as "HEY BOZO" and pointing out in syncopated fashion the folly of driving to work (fig. 9).[51]

Other issues, like homelessness, offer no apparently effective individual response. Sandy Straus's 1988 billboard based on the image of Joyce Brown, aka Billy Boggs (who was made famous briefly for refusing to be institutionalized during Mayor Koch's campaign to remove the mentally ill homeless from the streets of New York City) pointedly asked *How Do You HELP The Homeless?* (fig. 10).[52]

The AIDS Campaign

"*AIDS does not exist apart from the practices that conceptualize it, represent it, and respond to it.*" Douglas Crimp

AIDS may be the most prominent subject of artists' billboards of the past decade, and *Kissing Doesn't Kill, Greed and Indifference Do,* one of the most memorable images (fig. 11).[53] Created by Gran Fury (the graphics collective whose name refers to the Plymouth model once

FIG. 10 **Sandy Straus,** *How Do You HELP the Homeless,* billboard, 1988. Courtesy of the artist.

used by New York City police undercover cars), it unambiguously appropriated the 'multi-culti' models used by Bennetton as well as their wellknown advertising format to depict three mixed-race kissing couples of various sexual preferences.[54] Effectively following established commercial practices, Gran Fury launched aggressive advertising campaigns that, in addition to billboards, included posters, placards, T-shirts, stickers, and buttons with militant messages.[55] As advertisers had long realized, repetition works.

Formal Strategies

Artists' billboards enter the visual culture of the road at risk of invisibility.[56] Occupying a space defined by – and therefore as – advertising, they must capture the viewer's attention and 'sell' an idea rather than a product. In the time frame of a passing glance, they must create a visual stop, leaving the viewer with a thought to ponder rather than an image to buy. To accomplish this, artists used a variety of strategies: attacking billboards directly with graffiti; appropriating known ads only to change their meaning; creating structures that looked and functioned like billboards but weren't; using words only, images only, or a combination of words and images sufficiently different from advertising prototypes as to not be confused with them.

Subverting the Message

Artists who deface billboards with graffiti challenge their message directly.[57] Some, like Mark Pauline, who substituted a sinister message for a sales pitch, considered his broadly based "billboard modifications" pranks.[58] Other attacks were more issue oriented. In 1979 Jill Posener photographed a series of British billboards that were covered with graffiti pertaining to women's rights. On a London ad for a Fiat that read "If it were a lady, it would get its bottom pinched" someone added the words "If this lady was a car she'd run you down."[59]

A different kind of transformation is one that appropriates a specific recognizable ad, altering it sufficiently to both undercut the apparent meaning of the original and deliver a politically pointed message.

Like Gran Fury, David Collins and his helpers (known as Saatchi and Someone) altered other Benetton ads in Britain, 'refacing' rather than defacing. One depicted two attractive young women, one blond and white, the other black, holding an Asian baby between them next to the caption, "Lesbian mothers are everywhere."[60] While it may be too much to claim, as Liz McQuiston does, that, "Defacing and graffiti magically transform" billboards "into a two-way conversation" in which "the voice of authority is overtaken by the voice of resistance, and commercial power is subverted to people's power," these illegal attacks certainly undermine the ads they alter.[61]

Alternative Structures

A structure that looks (and seems to function) like a billboard but isn't is also an attention-getting device. In 1983 Mierle Laderman Ukeles mirrored the entire surface of a Department of Sanitation (garbage) truck.[62] *The Social Mirror*, an ingenious form of moving billboard with constantly changing images, involved the public, at least visually, in the sanitation process.

Karen Giusti created a 12'-deep billboard-like construction that read like a two-dimensional surface as you drove past. Her 1995 *The Green White House* depicted the White House in front and a dollar bill in back (fig. 12). Actually containing a greenhouse with potted perennials, the billboard, near the Connecticut Resources Recovery Authority in Hartford, turned green as the plants grew.[63]

Words Only

Since most advertising billboards consist of images and words, one signal that something other than advertising is happening is the use of words (or images) alone. To attract attention and prompt the viewer to actually read a words-only message, artists often use unusual compositions.

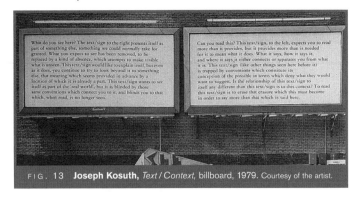

FIG. 13 **Joseph Kosuth,** *Text / Context,* billboard, 1979. Courtesy of the artist.

In 1979 Joseph Kosuth employed paired billboards and a lengthy text to signal a distinctly non-advertising message (fig. 13).[64] A decade later Felix Gonzalez-Torres created an AIDS billboard in a stream of consciousness series of phrases and dates without punctuation.[65] Displayed in New York's Greenwich Village, printed in white on black in two lines across the bottom, it read *People with AIDS Coalition 1985 Police Harassment 1969 Oscar Wilde 1895 Supreme/ Court 1986 Harvey Milk 1977 March on Washington 1987 Stonewall Rebellion 1969* (fig. 14).

Images Only

If words alone are a difficult strategy, images alone are perhaps even more so. The idea of letting a valent image speak for itself may have its roots in Andy

FIG. 14 **Felix Gonzalez-Torres,** *Untitled,* billboard, 1979. Photo: Stanley Greenberg. Courtesy of Public Art Fund.

FIG. 15 **Dennis Adams,** *Bus Shelter II, bus shelter* billboard, 1986. Photo: Peter Bellamy. Courtesy of Public Art Fund.

Warhol's depictions of electric chairs and car crashes. But if the image is not familiar, the meaning may be misread or not register with the audience at all. It is questionable whether Dennis Adams' photographic images of convicted spies Ethel and Julius Rosenberg taken at the time of their arrest in 1950 were still sufficiently recognizable to the larger public that saw *Bus Shelter II* in New York City in 1986 (fig. 15).[66] By conflating the private subject and the public arena, Felix Gonzalez-Torres' black and white photographic image of an empty bed – pillows and sheets with a just slept-in look, addressing AIDS and loss, was more likely to prompt curiosity (fig. 16).[67] But the viewer may be both too near (in terms of the focus) and too far (in terms of actual and symbolic space) to grapple with its disturbing anonymity. Does the emptiness become a universal metaphor for intimate, personal loss, a specter hovering around the edges of public consciousness, or is the viewer left wondering who is advertising these sheets?

Words and Images

More than any other artist, "media sculptor" Les Levine has experimented with formal variations of words and images, the building blocks of most billboards.[68] Using simplified images that lack the high gloss and perfection of advertising, Levine emphasized the disjunction between word and image (in a strategy made

FIG. 16 **Felix Gonzalez-Torres,** *Untitled,* (Bed), billboard, 1991. Photo: Stanley Greenberg. Courtesy of Public Art Fund.

famous by Magritte) in a 1983 inner city billboard campaign in Minneapolis, that juxtaposed, for instance, "RACE" with a picture of a horse (fig. 17).[69] Two years later, Levine combined images based on photographs he had taken in Northern Ireland with loaded words *(Blame, Kill, Attack, Torture,* and *Bomb)* followed by *God* (fig. 18).[70] Sited in

London, Derry, and Dublin, where the fighting in Northern Ireland is often referred to as a religious war, they were meant to shock and they did. Whether the response transferred from the images to the issues they raised is difficult to determine.

Future Formats?

In art and advertising, new technologies of necessity lead to new forms of expression.[71] James Fraser speculated in 1991 that with the use of fiber optics, future billboards might resemble a television screen with easily changeable images.[72] In 1998 a clip in *The New York Times* reported "new lighting technologies – some powerful enough to turn a whole building into a billboard."[73] But whatever form they take and whatever strategies they employ, the perception of a billboard is to a large extent determined by its site. Although there are arguably as many different viewing experiences as there are sites, certain broad distinctions exist.

FIG. 18 **Les Levine,** *Attack God,* billboard, 1985-86. Courtesy of the artist.

FIG. 17 **Les Levine,** *Race,* billboard design, 1983. Courtesy of the artist.

Variables of location determine viewing time and visual competition, as well as contexts of meaning.

Viewers on the Move

On the road, a billboard is seen from a moving vehicle, a focal point in an often familiar or apparently unchanging landscape, a welcome diversion unless, of course, there are too many. The moving consumer, dubbed an "auto-flâneur" by Kathleen Hulser, (relating him to nineteenth-century strollers taking in the sights of the then new urban metropolis), indulges in a form of visual cruising.[74]

In the city, transit slows down and pedestrians join the audience. But even with more time, in areas as dense as, say, Times Square, it may no longer be possible to sort out an image from the visual noise surrounding it.[75] From 1982 to 1990, *Message to the Public*, sponsored by the Public Art Fund, gave 114 artists the opportunity to experiment with the Spectacolor electronic light board located high on the building at 1 Times Square, one amidst many flashing signs for which the area was famous, to address a large audience on just about anything. I especially liked the billboard that asked *Have you sold your soul?* from the series by Komar and Melamid: *We Buy and Sell Souls* (fig. 19).

In 1993 and 1994, for a brief moment, before the most recent transformation of Times Square was complete, Creative Time included billboards in the projects they sponsored on 42nd Street between Broadway and Eighth Avenue.[76] But with the renovation of Times Square and new tenants like the Walt Disney Store and some of the giant financial firms that formerly resided on Wall Street, we can expect more spectacular building-size billboards, along with moving stock market quotes.[77] What will then be visible (i.e. seen or received) is anybody's guess. What seems certain, though, is that no affordable space will be available for art.

FIG. 19 **Komar and Melamid,** *Komar & Melamid, Inc. We buy and sell souls "Have you sold your soul?,"* billboard, 1978-79. Courtesy of the artists.

Stationary Viewers, Moving Billboards

Be it commuters waiting for mass transit or at a stoplight, or spectators sitting at a ballpark, stationary viewers are for a brief time a captive audience.[78] With a billboard on a moving bus (or other vehicle), it is the image rather than the viewer that moves, recreating at an accelerated rate the original experience of advertising boards carried around on foot. In either case, with repeated sightings possible, more subtle messages and strategies may have the time to resonate.

Location Matters

Specific location determines a context of meaning. Alfredo Jaar's billboard addressing First World/Third World issues in the pervasive geocentric reference to the United States as America was received differently in New York and Miami. Jaar created his multi-image, 45-second *A Logo for America* in 1987 as a Spectacolor billboard project for the Public Art Fund's *A Message to the Public* in Times Square (fig. 20).[79] The message, apparently clear (or just part of the overall contentious noise) in New York City, became problematic

FIG. 20 **Alfredo Jaar,** *A Logo for America,* Spectacolor billboard, 1987. Coutesy of Public Art Fund.

when Jaar displayed a *This is not America* billboard in and around Miami. With tensions among the Hispanic and Anglo populations still an issue, and differing interpretations of the phrase possible in Spanish, the message created an unintended controversy.[80] Just as specific locations determine meaning, so do temporal circumstances. *The Subject Is War* (fig. 21), a 1991 bus shelter billboard project in New Orleans created by Jan Gilbert working with Debra Howell, Marcel Lesseaux, and Kristen Struebing-Beazley,[81] was scheduled to coincide with the National Conference for Photographic Education. Unexpectedly, the Gulf War, then becoming a controversial reality, provided a specific context that prompted the leasing agency, fearing a violent reaction, to reject

seven of the eight works intended to address war in general. Although Gilbert worked with the patron to edit the images, she also created an exhibition, *The Subject Is War / The Subject Is Censorship* to display the original censored works, official objections, and subsequent modifications.[82]

Framing Artists' Billboards

Artists' billboards are clearly part of visual culture.[83] But are they art or advertising, and how meaningful is this distinction today? Lawrence Alloway as early as 1959 proposed considering art and mass media as a continuum.[84] Given the constant exchange and recycling of images, how can one see it differently? As one critic describing Walker Evans's photographs of billboards observed, "They are advertisements become photographs become posters become art."[85] Reflecting yet again the ability of capitalism to absorb anything, many artists' careers rest on their critical social work, admirable or politically correct (depending on your perspective), but in any case marketable. What then is the distinction between a public service message created by a 'fine' artist or someone working for an ad agency? If advertising is "fated to serve as the iconography of mass production and the corporate system," as Jackson Lears suggests, where does that leave commercially sponsored

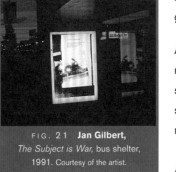

FIG. 21 **Jan Gilbert,** *The Subject is War,* bus shelter, 1991. Courtesy of the artist.

billboards that may raise issues as well as sales?[86] (Is selling goods so different from selling reputations?)

And what about audience awareness?[87] Is the populace a mindless miasma receptive to any propaganda, or is there a savvy citizenry out there, neither easily manipulated nor seduced? As with most either/or constructions, the truth lies more readily in less monolithic, more nuanced definitions.

Artists' billboards, included in exhibitions and funded by art agencies, have been framed largely as art.[88] Although they may seem anonymous to a general audience, signature styles are recognizable to the cognoscenti. Certainly billboards that are part of exhibitions are likely to be reviewed as art. But artists who approach billboards the way they make gallery art do so at risk.

Strategic Pitfalls

Art billboards may be less effective than their commercial counterparts because many artists fail to take into account the nature of their audience.[89] Although the general public may be intelligent, capable of critical judgment, they are rarely art-informed or familiar with the conventions of contemporary art. Considering the relative absence of art in our public education system, the greatest strategic pitfall when it comes to artists' billboards today would seem to be irony.

An accepted postmodern attitude, irony is an in-joke. You have to catch the tone and recognize the reference. While intending to undercut the dominant discourse, it may instead exclude (and alienate) the very audience it seeks to address (and convince). David Hammons's 1989 billboard image of a white, blond, blue-eyed Jesse Jackson, *How Ya Like Me Now*, was attacked by a group of young black men moments after it was installed in a downtown parking lot in Washington, D.C.[90]

If irony is questionable, humor is not. Examples like *Hey Bozo* are a reminder that levity may go a lot further than the alarmist tone of the evening news. The high road taken traditionally by critical art is not the highway. Current nostalgia for commercial signs of the road – images of a consumer culture defined largely by advertising (for better or worse) – also reflects their visual appeal.[91] As George Cukor's earnest but naive Gladys knew instinctively, billboards seduce. In the hands of sophisticated artists, they may have the power to transform.

CODA

"I think what makes a good billboard work is that you feel the information was meant for you ... when a lover blows a kiss you don't look over your shoulder ... By nature all public media has to generate some form of visual heat. Either it dissipates and cools off in the environment or is heated further by contact." Les Levine

1. I have had the benefit of many enlightening and entertaining conversations in developing this essay. My thanks especially to Michele Bogart, Rich Leslie, and Kathleen Hulser; Poyin Auyeung who wrote an excellent paper on billboards for a graduate seminar on public art controversy at the Graduate Center of the City University of New York during spring 1998; Melissa Sprague and Wendi Furman, my research assistants that semester; the staff at the Museum of Modern Art (MoMA) library, especially Jennifer Tobias; and Laura Raincovich at the Public Art Fund.

2. My thanks to Mary Lee Bandy at the Museum of Modern Art for this billboard reference.

3. See, for example, David Bernstein, *Advertising Outdoors: Watch This Space!* (London: Phaidon Press, 1997); James Fraser, *The American Billboard: 100 Years* (New York: Harry N. Abrams, 1991); Sally Henderson, *Billboard Art* (San Francisco: Chronicle Books, 1980). See also Dawn Ades, *The Twentieth Century Poster: Design of the Avant-Garde* (New York: Abbeville Press, 1984), a publication in conjunction with an exhibition of the same name at the Walker Art Center in Minneapolis and Mildred Friedman et al, *Graphic Design in America: A Visual Language History* (New York: Abrams, 1989), also a publication in conjunction with an exhibition of the same name at the Walker Art Center. The distinction between posters and billboards is examined most provocatively by Michele H. Bogart, *Artists, Advertising, and the Borders of Art* (Chicago: University of Chicago Press, 1995), pp. 79-124.

4. In Europe the word 'hoarding' was initially used to designate a temporary fence around a building that was often used to display ads and eventually came to signify a structure for displaying advertising, comparable to the American billboard.

5. A billboard is defined as "a large outdoor board or hoarding for advertisements" in *The New Shorter Oxford English Dictionary*, Lesley Brown, ed. (Oxford: Clarendon Press, 1993) p. 227. Kirk Varnedoe and Adam Gopnik, *High & Low: Modern Art and Popular Culture* (New York: Museum of Modern Art, 1990) explored the influence of words, graffiti, caricature, comics and advertising on modern art. It includes illustrations of Eugene Atget's photographs of early twentieth century Paris buildings covered with advertising posters.

6. Interestingly, the word poster was used initially to designate a person who put up notices (i.e. a bill poster) and then the printed or written notice that was posted.

7. Robert Brown, "Posters at the Turn of the Century," in Dawn Ades, *The Twentieth Century Poster*, p. 15.

8. I am grateful to Matthew Affron for references to the literature on billboards in France that continued well into the 1920s and '30s, including artists' debates (Cocteau et al) and a larger body of literary meditations including Apollinaire and Blaise Cendrars. See especially, A.M. Cassandre, *Le Spectacle est dans la rue* (Paris: Draeger Freres, 1936) and *Art et publicité 1890-1990* (Paris: Centre Georges Pompidou, 1990).

9. Mildred Friedman, "Broadside to Billboard," in Dawn Ades, *The Twentieth Century Poster*, p. 10. Broadside, the joining of two words, broad and side, originally signifying the side of a ship and a type of attack, also refers to a broadsheet, "a large sheet of paper carrying information printed on one side only." (*Oxford*, p. 286)

10. See Magdalena Dabrowski, et al, *Aleksandr Rodchenko*, (New York: Museum of Modern Art, 1998). A number of interesting interpretations of Constructivism and its aftermath are found in *Art Into Life: Russian Constructivism 1914-1932* (Seattle, WA: The Henry Art Gallery with Rizzoli, 1990).

11. Bogart, p. 89.

12. See William H. Wilson, "The Billboard: Bane of the City Beautiful," *Journal of Urban History*, v. 13, n. 4, Aug. 1987, pp. 394-425. The following section is largely indebted to this thoughtful thoroughly documented study.

13. Wilson, p. 396.

14. For a summary of a 1911 opinion upholding billboard control see John J. Costonis, *Icons and Aliens: Law, Aesthetics, and Environmental Change* (Urbana and Chicago: University of Illinois, 1989), p. 23. Billboards were described as "constant menaces to the public safety and welfare of the city; they endanger public health, promote immorality, constitute hiding places and retreats for criminals and classes of miscreants – the evidence shows – that the ground in the rear thereof is being constantly used as privies and dumping grounds for all kinds of waste and deleterious matters, and...behind these obstructions the lowest form of prostitution and other acts of immorality are frequently carried on, almost under the public gaze." Similar arguments were made in the 1970s and '80s against radically different public sculpture by George Sugarman and Richard Serra. See Harriet F. Senie, "Richard Serra's `Tilted Arc': Art and Non-Art Issues," *Art Journal,* Winter 1989, pp. 298-302.

15. Wilson, p. 408. The political implications of these billboard wars are analyzed in Bogart, pp. 89-119.

16. Wilson, p. 420.

17. For an interesting summary of the visual experience of modern artists, see George H. Roeder, Jr., "What Have Modernists Looked At? Experiential Roots of Twentieth-Century American Painting," *American Quarterly 39* (Spring 1987), pp. 54-83.

18. Jackson Lears, "Uneasy Courtship: Modern Art and Modern Advertising," *American Quarterly 39* (Spring 1987), pp. 133-54. Although he argues for the profound difference between art and advertising, he also observes (p. 151) that "it is difficult to escape the conclusion that much of the profoundest twentieth-century art has defined itself – at least unconsciously – against the symbolic universe of advertising."

19. Wanda M. Corn, *In the American Grain: The Billboard Poetics of Charles Demuth* (Poughkeepsie: Vassar College, 1989), p. 13.

20. Corn, p. 11, describes billboard cubism as "a style that brings together cubo-futurist compositional devices with the bluntness, scale, modern typography, and legibility of 1920s posters and billboards. Billboard cubism self-consciously fused the high principles of modernism with the lowbrow practices of street signage."

21. Corn, pp. 10, 17.

22. See, for example, *Walker Evans' SIGNS* (Los Angeles, The J. Paul Getty Museum, 1998), with an essay by Andrei Codrescu.

23. Codrescu, p. 6.

24. James Fraser, *The American Billboard: 100 Years* (New York: Harry N. Abrams, 1991), p. 16.

25. Fraser, p. 24.

26. Wilson, p. 419. Bogart, p. 105, cites the industry's war effort as marking the (temporary) turning point in public support for outdoor advertising.

27. Fraser, p. 30.

28. Bernstein, pp. 34-35, discusses this European view of American clients, noting that even the more modern graphic designer Otis Shepard also complained about "the pretty girl mania" in the United States.

29. William L. Bird, Jr., and Harry R. Rubenstein, *Design for Victory: World War II Posters on the American Home Front* (New York: Princeton Architectural Press, 1998), p. 1. My subsequent discussion of World War II posters depends largely on their work.

30. Bird and Rubenstein, p. 9.

31. Bird and Rubenstein, p. 21, 25. The Office of War Information (OWI) developed six themes: the nature of the enemy, the nature of our allies, the need to work, the need to fight, the need to sacrifice, and the Americans as "fighting for the four freedoms, the principles of the Atlantic Charter, Democracy, and no discrimination against races and religions," pp. 32-36.

32. Bird and Rubenstein, p. 44.

33. Although the Pop artists themselves don't appear to have created any billboards (they were, after all, escaping from the world of advertising, seeking alternative sites for their art), it is interesting to note that Richard Hamilton's famous collage of 1956, "*Just what is it that makes today's homes so appealing,*" was actually designed for reproduction in a catalogue and a poster. See, for example, Lynne Cooke, "The Independent Group: British and American Pop Art, a 'Palimpcestuous' Legacy," in Kirk Varnedoe and Adam Gopnik, eds., *Modern Art and Popular Culture: Readings in High & Low* (New York: The Museum of Modern Art and Harry N. Abrams, 1991), p. 192. Although British Pop Art predated its appearance in the United States, the movement is so identified with this country that I will limit subsequent references to its American manifestation.

34. For a good summary of the criticism of Pop, see Carol Anne Mahsun, *Pop Art: The Critical Dialogue* (Ann Arbor: UMI Research Press, 1989).

35. My thanks to Rich Leslie for this reference.

36. For example, Roland Barthes, "That Old Thing, Art –" in Paul Taylor, ed, *Post-Pop Art* (Cambridge, MA: The MIT Press, 1989), observes, "Pop Art – accepts being an imagery, a collection of reflections, constituted by the banal reverberation of the American environment – Pop Art's objective – is neither metaphoric nor metonymic, it presents itself cut off from its source and its surroundings," p. 21, 25.

37. Jean Baudrillard, "Pop – An Art of Consumption?" in Taylor, *Post-Pop Art*, p. 42, suggests that a response to pop "requires neither aesthetic ecstasy nor effective or symbolic participation ('deep involvement'), but a kind of abstract involvement, or instrumental curiosity." But it is that curiosity precisely which translates into a "what does that mean?" experience rather than "what is it?" that leads the viewer into a decidedly queasy state of questioning and keeps pop from wearing what Baudrillard defines as "the smile of collusion," p. 44.

38. Peter Blake, *God's Own Junkyard: The Planned Deterioration of America's Landscape* (New York: Holt, Rinehart and Winston, 1964), p. 8.

39. Robert Venturi, *Complexity and Contradiction in Architecture* (New York, The Museum of Modern Art, 1966).

40. Robert Venturi, Denise Scott Brown, Steven Izenour, *Learning from Las Vegas: The Forgotten Symbolism of Architectural Form* (Cambridge, MA: The MIT Press, 1972), p. 6.

41. For the evolution of recent public sculpture see Harriet F. Senie, *Contemporary Public Sculpture* (New York: Oxford University Press, 1992).

42. One notable exception from the political billboard is the Alabama Artists Outdoor projects which enlarged works of local artists to billboard size. This project, originated by the Alabama State Council on the Arts with space and production assistance provided by Alabama Outdoor Advertising, Lamar Advertising, Jennings Outdoor, and Durden Outdoor "to increase public awareness of the work of visual artists within the state," in effect advertised art. It was recognized as a "direct promotion of Alabama artists and their works to a statewide and regional audience." Although the examples of this public/private enterprise appear far from noteworthy, the project remains an interesting idea. See Kathy Holland, "Taking Art to the Streets," *Alabama Arts,* Spring 1994, pp. 13-15.

43. Liz McQuiston, *Graphic Agitation: Social and Political Graphics Since the Sixties* (London: Phaidon Press, 1993), p. 19, suggests that the 1900-1920 women's suffrage campaign was "probably the first to borrow styles and techniques of commercial advertising posters to serve a distinct political cause or anti-establishment viewpoint."

44. For a critical overview of the Guerrilla Girls see Elizabeth Hess, "Guerrilla Girl Power: Why the Art World Needs a Conscience," in Nina Felshin, ed., *But Is It Art? The Spirit of Art as Activism* (Seattle: Bay Press, 1995), pp. 309-32.

45. Initially refused billboard space in New York in the late '80s, the Guerrilla Girls displayed this image in their illegal posters and a bus ad. See McQuiston, p. 169.

46. In 1970-71 the ad agency Cramer Saatchi (less effectively) used a literal image of a pregnant man over the caption, "Would you be more careful if it was you that got pregnant?" Created for the British Health Education Council, it is illustrated in McQuiston, p. 176. For an overview of Kruger's work see Kate Linker, *Love for Sale: The Words and Pictures of Barbara Kruger* (New York: Harry N. Abrams, 1990). See also W.J.T. Mitchell, "An Interview with Barbara Kruger," in W.J.T. Mitchell, ed., *Art and the Public Sphere* (Chicago: The University of Chicago Press, 1990), pp. 235-48.

47. This series was sponsored by the Public Art Fund. In one version, a bluecollar worker, helmet on head, hands in pocket, asks "We've finally sent the kids off to school. We're not getting any younger. I've got high blood pressure and arthritis. I just found out I'm pregnant. What should I do?" In another, a yuppie-looking white man dressed in a suit, arms crossed, ponders, "I've worked hard. Business is booming and I've decided to enter politics. The campaign is going really well but I just found out I'm pregnant. What should I do?" It was part of a larger project entitled *PSA: Public Service Art* that also included a billboard by the Guerrilla Girls, subway posters by Ann Meredith, and bus shelter posters by Gran Fury.

48. Founded in 1979 by 12 artists and writers, the group's original members included Doug Ashford, Julie Ault and Felix Gonzalez-Torres. They identified their principle focus as democracy and AIDS, and practiced inclusionary and alternative curatorial strategies in their gallery on East 13th Street, New York (opened in 1980) and subsequent ventures.

In this project they worked in collaboration with the (now defunct) Randolph Street Gallery and Gannett Advertising. For a detailed discussion of the evolution of Group Material see Jan Avgikos, "Group Material Timeline: Activism as a Work of Art," in Nina Felshin, ed., *But Is It Art?*, pp. 85-116. See also Trevor Fairbrother and Kathryn Potts, *In and Out of Place: Contemporary Art and the American Social Landscape* (Boston: Museum of Fine Arts, 1993), pp. 41-48.

49. This account of the project is based on an oral presentation by Julie Ault at MASS MoCA on October 31, 1998. See also McQuiston, p. 183.

50. My thanks to Wendy Feuer for this reference. Other billboards in the project include Helja Keading's image of a child with a gas mask on a congested highway over the caption, "Carbon Monoxide is a Lethal Gas" (*MTA News release*, #97, Oct. 1, 1990); and Roger Shimomura's cars covered by black clouds exhorting viewers to "Use Mass Transit" (*MTA News release*, #7, Jan. 21, 1992).

51. The entire text read: "HEY BOZO/You drive to work/get stuck in traffic/have an accident/get three parking tickets in one day/you drive home like everyone else/stalled in gridlock/choking on fumes/you arrive home tenser than RAMBO on a mission/next day/you drive to work/get stuck in traffic/a truck cuts you off/you fight with the driver/you're late for work/ your car is towed/you spend 150 bucks to get it back/you arrive home with a migraine the size of Minneapolis/day in/day out/it's the same/what are you/a clown/USE MASS TRANSIT." See *MTA News release,* #54, May 5, 1994.

52. Straus's hand painted billboard, sponsored by Steven Style and the gallery Fashion Moda appeared in five locations in Manhattan.

53. In 1987 a window installation at the New Museum in New York, *Let the Record Show*, featured quotes by Jesse Helms, Jerry Falwell, William F. Buckley, and many others, as well as the slogan "Silence = Death" in a pink triangle, the emblem of gay liberation since the sixties. Created by the activist group ACT UP, it marked the realization for many that to be effective, activist art had to reach beyond art world confines. See Douglas Crimp, ed., *AIDS Cultural Analysis/Cultural Activism* (Cambridge: MIT Press, 1988). In that year an exhibition at the Museum of Modern Art, *Committed to Print: Social and Political Themes in Recent American Art* omitted any work pertaining to AIDS.

54. Part of the 1989 exhibition, *Art Against AIDS/On The Road,* that premiered in San Francisco, it elicited considerable controversy in other cities. See, for example, *Arts Magazine,* Nov. 1990, p. 122.

55. See Douglas Crimp and Adam Ralston, *AIDS Demographics* (Seattle, Bay Press, 1990) for a discussion of ACT UP and its various graphic expressions. The book is "presented as a do-it-yourself manual, showing how to make propaganda work in the fight against AIDS," p. 13.

56. For a discussion of the larger problem of the role of art amidst the visual cacophony that defines contemporary society, see Catherine Gudis, ed., *A Forest of Signs: Art in the Crisis of Representation* (Cambridge, MA: The MIT Press, 1989), an exhibition catalogue that includes essays by Mary Jane Jacob and Ann Goldstein.

57. More examples of graffiti attacks are cited in Laura Steward Heon's essay.

58. Pauline initially wanted to work in Florida, "the truly seminal land of billboards," but realized his ambition only after he moved to San Francisco. In 1979 he painted over a billboard in North Beach, California advertising Jeno's Italian Bread Pizza, changing the image of a friendly looking middle-aged man with glasses dressed in a suit to a masked face over a body with a jock strap holding a head next to the word 'Dead'

(instead of bread). For an account of Pauline's guerilla activities see Andrea Juno and Vale, eds., *Re/Search #11: Pranks!* (San Francisco: Re/Search Publications, 1987), pp. 6-17. My thanks to Laura Senie for this reference.

59. McQuiston, pp. 168-69. The author observed that Posener's photographs "were widely reproduced, and became symbolic of women's grassroots resistance against the public images that dominated their lives." See also, Lucy Lippard, *Get the Message? A Decade of Art for Societal Change* (New York: E.P.Dutton, 1984), pp. 201-10.

60. McQuiston, pp. 183, 205.

61. McQuiston, p. 182.

62. A few years earlier Ukeles shook hands with all New York City Sanitation Department employees and subsequently became the department's official artist-in-residence. For an interesting overview of Ukeles' projects see Patricia C. Phillips, "Maintenance Activity: Creating a Climate for Change," in Nina Felshin, ed, *But Is It Art? The Spirit of Art as Activism* (Seattle: Bay Press, 1995), pp. 165-193.

63. According to Giusti, she intended to demonstrate that government investment is necessary to develop new energy sources. For commentary on the project see John Lacy, "A Hothouse of American Ingenuity," *The Hartford Courant,* August 30, 1995; and Patricia Rostoff, "The Greening of the White House," *The Hartford Advocate*, Aug. 10, 1995, p. 25. The project was presented a year later in 1996 at Battery Park, New York City by the Lower Manhattan Cultural Council.

64. In conjunction with an exhibition at Leo Castelli Gallery titled *Text/Context,* Joseph Kosuth created a series of billboards in various locations: New York, Edinburgh, Cologne, and Genoa, each with its own message. The New York version consisted of two billboards side by side, one beginning with the question "What do you see here?" the other "Can you read this?" For a discussion of his work see Joseph Kosuth, *Art After Philosophy and After: Collected Writings, 1966-1990* (Cambridge: The MIT Press, 1991).

65. Clare Farrow, ed., *Ad Reinhardt Joseph Kosuth Felix Gonzales-Torrez: Symptoms of Interference, Conditions of Possibility* (London: Academy Group Ltd, 1994) related the work of these three artists. Gonzales-Torrez discusses the exhibition in an interview with Robert Storr, "Felix Gonzalez-Torres, Being a Spy," *Artpress,* Jan. 1995, pp. 24-32.

66. For an interesting analysis of Adams' work see Mary Anne Staniszewski, *Dennis Adams: The Architecture of Amnesia* (New York: Kent Gallery, 1990), p. 10.

67. The billboards, sponsored by the Public Art Fund, were installed in 24 New York City locations around the city in 1991 in conjunction with the artist's exhibition at the Museum of Modern Art *Projects 34: Felix Gonzales-Torres*. For a discussion of this work see Nancy Spector, *Felix Gonzalez-Torres* (New York: Guggenheim Museum, 1995), pp. 23-25.

68. Levine considers himself a "media sculptor, … someone who works with the media the way other people work with paint, bronze, wood …" and calls his work "media art." Interview with Declan McGonagle in *Blame God: Billboard Propositions* (London: Institute of Contemporary Art, 1985), p. 42. See also Holland Cotter's catalogue essay, "Wise, Audacious and True," in *Crazy Wisdoms B & Z: Computer Assisted Silkscreens by Les Levine* (Ossining, NY: Elizabeth Galasso Editions, 1986), p. 2.

69. Other billboards juxtaposed AIM with a deer head; TAKE with a crane; STEAL with a factory, and FORGET with four elephants.

70. These billboards were created as part of an exhibition at the Institute of Contemporary Art (ICA) in London. For an analysis of Levine's linguistic strategy see Thomas McEvilley, "The Collaboration of Word and Image in The Art of Les Levine," *Blame God: Billboard Propositions* (London: Institute of Contemporary Art, 1985).

71. See, for example, Estelle Jussim, "Changing Technology Changes Design," in Mildred Friedman, *Graphic Design in America*, pp. 105-17.

72. Fraser, p. 187. Bernstein, pp. 176-220, also speculates on the future of the commercial billboard.

73. "Lighting: Turning a Building Into a Billboard," *The New York Times,* Dec. 24, 1998, p. F3. The clip continued, "Now almost anything can be advertised upon. (Expect new laws.)"

74. Kathleen Hulser, "Visual Browsing: Auto-flâneurs and Roadside Ads in the 1950s," in Peter Lang and Tom Miller, eds., *Suburban Discipline* (Princeton: Princeton Architectural Press, 1997).

75. The Great White Way, darkened during World War II both to conserve energy and avoid illuminating a possible target, reemerging from darkness as a sign of celebration now inseparable from New Year's Eve, remains the urban epitome of visual over-excitement. For a history of the signs of Times Square, see Tama Starr and Edward Hayman, *Signs and*

Wonders: The Spectacular Marketing of America (New York: Doubleday, 1998).

76. Creative Time (an independent public art agency), and the 42nd Street Development Project, Inc., in cooperation with the City's Economic Development Corporation, published brochures documenting these projects, which were subsequently reviewed in the art press. Projects included a movie marquee with words from Jenny Holzer's *Truism* and *Survival* series, a billboard with the ever popular image of the Cat in the Hat by Theodore Geisel (Dr. Seuss), and a billboard by Tibor Kalman and Scott Stowell with the word EVERYBODY writ large over variously colored mounted chairs, exactly on the site where the police information center used to be.

77. The entire May 18, 1997, issue of *The New York Times Magazine* was devoted to the changing faces of Times Square. See also Charles V. Bagli, "Bullish on Times Square Neon: Wall Street Muscles Into Mecca of Commercial Glitter," *The New York Times,* Aug. 20, 1998, pp. B1,B6; Doug Stewart, "Times Square Reborn," *Smithsonian,* Feb. 1998, pp. 34-44. Tibor Kalman, "Your Ad Here," *The New York Times,* May 22, 1998, p. A25, speculates, "Strolling Manhattan could become worse than watching television. Only you can't turn a skyscraper off."

78. One selection of Jenny Holzer's electronic messages 1987 *Survival Series,* "You Must Have ONE Grand Passion," was displayed at Candlestick Park in San Francisco surrounded by a scoreboard, the Giants logo and ads for beer and cigarettes. For a critique see Jed Perl, "Jenny Holzer: Billboards," *Modern Painters,* 1990, v. 3, n.2, pp. 46-47.

79. The images included a map of the United States; the words "This is not America" over the outline of the map; the American flag; "This is not America's flag" over the outline of the flag; and the word AMERICA with a map of North and South America in place of the letter E. For a discussion of this and other projects, see Madeleine Grynsztejn, *Alfredo Jaar* (La Jolla, CA: La Jolla Museum of Contemporary Art, 1990)

80. See Susan Valdes-Dapena, "Miami No Es Los Estados Unidos," *Art Papers,* Nov-Dec. 1998, pp. 22-23. A comparably problematic response might have occurred, she suggests, if Jaar's billboard had been displayed in a neighborhood such as Harlem or Bedford-Stuyvesant.

81. Working as the Vestiges Project (New Orleans-based group of visual artists and writers since 1984 whose purpose is to "investigate the inter-connection of image and text and aim to produce work that transcends the purely verbal and visual") they realized this project in conjunction with a local leasing agency, Transportation Displays, Inc. (TDI). It consisted of a series of images of words and texts representative of different voices or perspectives (children, soldiers, statistics, etc.).

82. See Alice Thorson, "Censored?" *The Kansas City Star,* Mar 28, 1993, p. J-5, for a discussion of the project.

83. John A. Walker and Sarah Chaplin, *Visual Culture: An Introduction* (Manchester: Manchester University Press, 1997), p. 2 define visual culture as "material artifacts, buildings and images, plus time-based media and performances, produced by human labor and imagination, which serve aesthetic, symbolic, ritualistic or ideological-political ends, and/or practical functions, and which address the sense of sight to a significant extent."

84. Lawrence Alloway's, "The Long Front of Culture," originally appearing in *Cambridge Opinion 17,* was reprinted ten years later in John Russell and Suzi Gablik, *Pop Art Redefined* (New York: Praeger, 1969), pp. 41-43. Special thanks to Rich Leslie for this reference and discussions of Alloway's role as a critic. In the same anthology

John McHale, "The Fine Arts in the Mass Media," pp. 43-47, discusses the various corporate uses of art. See also Maud Lavin, "Design in the Service of Commerce" in Friedman, *Graphic Design in America,* pp. 127-43.

85. Sara Boxer, "3 Degrees of Separation on the Road to Art," *The New York Times,* Aug. 7, 1998, p. E34.

86. Jackson Lears, "Uneasy Courtship: Modern Art and Modern Advertising," *American Quarterly,* Spring 1987, p. 141.

87. For a brief survey of significant theories of consumption, see John Storey, *Cultural Studies and the Study of Popular Culture: Theories and Methods* (Athens: University of Georgia Press, 1996), pp. 113-36.

88. See, for example, Nancy Marmer, "Documenta 8: The Social Dimension," *Art in America,* Sept. 1987, which included a billboard by Barbara Kruger, "In space no one can hear you scream." Marmer, p. 199, concluded, "Perhaps the reason that Documenta 8 is finally not a show of 'art about society' but, like its predecessors, about Western art in the Western art market: it is about individual artists, individual careers and individual marketable art works. The myths are all the same." See also Eleanor Heartney, "Report from Newcastle: Cultivating an Engaged Public Art," *Art in America,* Oct. 1990, pp. 53-57, for a review of the *First International Exhibition of Contemporary Art,* organized by Declan McGonagle in Gateshead and Newcastle, also addressing the problems of contemporary public art with a social focus. This exhibition included Chris Wainwright's billboard, *ALL THAT GLISTERS IS NOT GOLD,* bringing images of the Brazilian rain forest into this setting of a garden festival.

89. Nancy Roth, "'Artside Out': The Inside Story" *Afterimage,* Oct. 1985, p. 5, in reviewing an artists' billboard exhibition in St. Paul supported by local Firstbanks and the National Endowment for the Arts, and including works by John Baldessari, Barbara Kruger, and Martha Rosler, among others, observed that except for the contribution by William Wegman, the works weren't "billboards but simply large gallery images, [and therefore] they are overwhelmed by their circumstance." In a review of a 1988 censored billboard project in the UK, David Baggaley, "Politics, Patronage & Public Art," *Circa,* Dec. 1990, p. 32, observed that "public art" involves something more than simply bringing what was once 'private' (or otherwise surrounded by exclusions) out into the open." David Lee, "BBC Billboard Project," *Arts Review,* June 1992, pp. 234-35, concluded that in this project involving commissioned billboards from 15 artists including Howard Hodgkin, Richard Long and Damian Hirst, "fine artists no longer have the flair to compete in the real visual world."

90. This billboard, based on a long tradition of political campaign billboards, was one of seven outdoor installations in the exhibition, "The Blues Aesthetic: Black Culture and Modernism," by the WPA in Washington, D.C. The title was taken from a song by the performer Kool Moe Dee. Hammons eventually repaired the piece and added the hammers of destruction, thereby incorporating its problematic history. This incident and its implications were the subject of an unpublished talk I gave at the College Art Association annual meeting in 1994: "Conservative Styles, Radical Misreadings? Racial Content in Public Art by David Hammons, John Ahearn and Richard Haas." For a detailed discussion of Hammons' work see Steve Cannon, Kellie Jones, Tom Finkelpearl, *David Hammons: Rousing the Rabble* (Cambridge: The MIT Press, 1992).

91. For an insightful account of the evolution of our culture into a style-based or image-based construct, see Stuart Ewen, *All Consuming Images: The Politics of Style in Contemporary Culture* (New York: Basic Books, 1988).

BILLBOARD

Causing Conversations,
Taking
Positions

Peggy Diggs

It has always interested me, as a maker of art on billboards and in other ephemeral formats, that works of art demonstrating permanence, technical skill, and objecthood are valued much more highly than temporary forms, regardless of the ideas expressed. Much short-lived public art, of which the billboard is the most familiar form, is relatively inexpensive to produce, is sometimes made collaboratively with groups of non-artists, and is difficult to collect. Although the artist's billboard appears in a space dedicated to advertising, it cannot be commodified; such a billboard makes its point – usually to an unintentional audience – and then is gone.

Engaging with temporary public art as an artist and as a viewer is both troubling and exciting for me. I am riddled with questions that are tough to answer and sometimes impossible to clarify. As an artist committed to social change, I ask what responsibilities I have in public and to the public. What can I do in a public site and what should I not do? If I involve a community group through interviews or participation in other ways, but the group does not make the final decisions, whose piece is it? Is anyone being exploited? What responsibilities do I have to my collaborators? What might a group process be hiding – that is, what might it be pretending to do but not really doing? Is it possible to create a public piece without preaching or lecturing? What do I do about the possibility of misrepresentation? If I create work in a public site, who has authority over what is said or portrayed? Whose voice am I using and do I have the right to use it? If I work on a project that's meant to be educational, whose information should be put forward? How much should I tell an audience, and how do I justify my answer? How do I measure the effectiveness of my project? How do I determine success? When I make work about social issues, how do I or should I elicit responsible responses? How do I reconcile the gap between whom I want to reach with my work and whom I reach in practice? A viewer might deal with many of the same questions and might also wonder where the edge between art and social work lies. When is a project 'art' and does it matter? What baggage do artists take to various sites (such as advertising billboards) that might interfere with the point of the project? Which sites are appropriate for public discourse? And what can really be accomplished by art in a public site?

As an artist, a viewer, and now a curator of billboards, I am quite aware of the obstacles that must be overcome for an artist to successfully reach an accidental viewer. First, an artist must contend with the hubbub of the street, decide whether to blend in or stand out, and consider how that will affect the viewer's consideration of the design. Second, an artist has to grapple with what the viewer expects to see, which is generally advertising.

Third, an artist committed to social change must relate the billboard to the public in some way, rather than present a strictly private expression. Fourth, after the billboard has been mounted, the artist is often required (usually by funders) to identify the affected audience and to measure the impact of the work on that audience. (Artists working in other formats are not asked how many people saw their work or how many people's minds were affected or changed; but once in public venues, there are assumptions that the modes of consumption change.)

Some will say a principal reason why an artist might choose to leave the full authority of her own studio to make art in the highly restrictive space of a public billboard is to effect change. But

FIG. 1 **Peggy Diggs,** *Domestic Violence*, billboard, 1991. Courtesy of the artist.

consider how change happens at many workplaces; people often resist new proposals initially. Change occurs over time, through familiarity, trust, and trying something new in steps, over and over. If change is not apt to happen with a single proposal at your job, then neither will it happen with a single image or text on a billboard. So what might be the goals of the short-lived public art project? Perhaps, in the end, billboards (and other transient public artwork) may simply cause conversations, urge new thinking, or encourage a slight alteration in the way something is seen. That may be all the work can do.

If a billboard can serve as an excuse for dialogue between people, then I believe that may be its maximum achievement. Consider a billboard about domestic violence. In the fall of 1991, I installed a 10' x 20' billboard (fig. 1) in three locations (Pittsfield, Adams, and Lee, Massachusetts). The billboard had an image of a family, including a woman with a black eye, and text that read, "DOES HE HURT YOU?" My hope was that a battered woman could use the billboard to broach the subject with a friend or family member. In that discussion she might be able to feel out the tendency of her friend to blame the victim or to understand why a woman might find it difficult to leave the abuser; in other words, she could determine whether it was safe to discuss her own situation without fear of being condemned or abandoned. Even if the artwork gets ridiculed, it could serve as an excuse for conversation and position-taking between people.

Billboard art often instigates a process, a questioning, or an argument about an issue or value that often goes unquestioned or unresolved in the public mind. This sort of public art has a slightly different life than the usual presentation of information and opinions. People expect the billboard to be a site for advertising products, lifestyles, or services. But if an artist infiltrates the banal billboard format with another kind of communication – the 'wrong' message appearing in a familiar context – then a glitch in the viewer's assumptions might make her see this communication differently. This is how billboard art can cut through much of the white noise of our day.

Education theorist Henry Giroux said, "You can define democracy within the narrow limits of electoral politics, or you can define it as an ongoing contest within every aspect of daily life."[1] In a democracy, theoretically there is room for public discourse in that ongoing contest, but more often than not The Public is not a contestant. Rather, I think that the public is made of (and made to be by the dominant social paradigm) largely passive and unresponsive receivers, often because there is no forum for response. Perhaps, due to a feeling of ineffectiveness we may harbor as citizens, we may also have no desire to respond, no belief that our effort to engage in public discourse will effect social change.

This is why the artist's billboard and other temporary hit-and-run art projects have value. As art historian and public art theorist Patricia Phillips wrote:

> The temporary … permits art production to simulate the idea of the research laboratory. This proposal is conservative: a suggestion to take time, to study, to try more modest projects, to express what is known about the contemporary condition. It requires a comprehension of value based on ideas and content rather than on lasting forms, a flexibility of procedures for making and placing art, and a more inventive and attentive critical process.[2]

By removing a sustainable object that would serve as a mnemonic device for history, time, and particular values, the temporary public art project enters the fray of democracy.

These ephemeral public provocations and the conversations they instigate ultimately reveal who we are, what's important to us, where our respect lies, to what we feel responsible, and how we manifest these allegiances. As I surveyed billboard images for this exhibition and catalogue, I tried to apply my own concerns about public art to the selection process. As a result, many of these billboards urge new thinking about some of our society's basic tenets. It's in how we respond to these urgings, and how we discuss our responses with friends and neighbors, that we put these works to work. With so much public space usurped by the media, corporate culture, and advertising, an effective public-art billboard is one of the few possible public sites from which dissent, transition, and halting steps toward resolution can germinate. At its best, an artist's billboard provides a space where citizens speak to citizens.

1. Trend, David. "Critical Pedagogy and Cultural Power: An Interview with Henry A. Giroux." *Border Crossings: Cultural Workers and the Politics of Education.* Henry Giroux, au. New York: Routledge, 1992, p. 155.

2. Phillips, Patricia C. "Temporality and Public Art." *Critical Issues in Public Art: Content, Context, and Controversy.* Harriet F. Senie and Sally Webster, eds. New York: Harper Collins, 1992, p. 298-299.

Billboards for the Berkshires

MASS MoCA commissioned Julie Ault and Martin Beck, Lothar Baumgarten, Sue Coe, Leon Golub, and Gary Simmons to create new billboards for its community. On a weekend during October 1998, most of the artists came to the region to acquaint themselves with Adams and North Adams and to meet with residents who shared their interests. That exchange resulted in these billboards, which were displayed in the two towns from May 30 through September 30, 1999.

daydreams &

Ault and Beck's billboard differs from the other commissioned works in that it is an iteration of their larger, ongoing project, *Outdoor Systems. Outdoor Systems* is not simply a series of works united by a theme; rather, it is a conceptual and methodological tool for investigating systems of signs with an emphasis on process, not product. In *daydreams &*, the artists consider both the physical location of billboards in the city and their metaphysical standing in this community. *Daydreams &* connects the specific situation in North Adams (a city in the midst of remaking itself) to the larger framework of American downtown revitalization efforts. In the billboard, an aerial view of downtown North Adams, somewhat obscured by the intense color, is coupled with an open-ended slogan, "daydreams & traffic jams," and a list of the stakeholders in the process of urban transformation. The billboard does not refer to literal traffic jams, of which there are few if any in this region, but to the heavy traffic of ideas and special interests in the process of revitalization.

While visiting North Adams, Beck and Ault met with representatives from North Adams, Adams, and Williamstown to discuss the different sign systems in the three communities. These conversations made the artists aware of how signage reflects the social and economic transformations the region is undergoing. The artists made two billboards for this exhibition, one for Adams and one (shown here) for North Adams, to underscore the notion of site as content that is central to their *Outdoor Systems* project.

stakeholders

economic development groups

preservationists

tra

property owners

media

bankers

consumers

elected and appointed officials

civic clubs

utility companies

business owners

residents

daydreams &

fic jams

curb your dogma

Lothar Baumgarten's wry *curb your dogma* was made in December 1998, in the midst of the impeachment hearings of President Clinton due to his adulterous affair with a White House intern, Monica Lewinsky; the suspiciously timed bombing of Iraq, which some insinuated was intended to draw attention away from the impeachment; and the resignation of the Republican Speaker-Designate of the House of Representatives, who had been an ardent critic of Clinton, due to his adulterous affair. The vociferousness of political attacks and counterattacks during this period tried the patience of the American people, who responded with disgruntled apathy.

Baumgarten's billboard speaks to the dogmatic element in us all, but more so to the media machine of which billboards are a part. The billboard's brief text (brevity being the soul of wit) relies entirely on the timeliness billboards so effectively provide.

our

dogma

Sue Coe

Billboards for
the Berkshires

Go Vegetarian

Made in consultation with a group of local animal rights activists, Sue Coe's billboard admonishes the viewer to "Go Vegetarian!" The starkness of Coe's social-realist style suits the gruesome scene: a haggard man on his deathbed, with a bloody hamburger on his bedside table, who is visited by the placid ghosts of animals he has eaten or whose skins he has worn. Coe draws on a long tradition of painters and graphic artists, such as Francisco Goya and Honore Daumier, who couple expressionistic realism with indignant politics.

Although Coe worked with local activists, the vegetarian politics expressed in this billboard are not site-specific. To mark the connection of this image to the region, Coe added a small painting of a well-known landmark, the war memorial on nearby Mount Greylock. In addition, she dedicated the billboard to the activists she spoke with in North Adams, including their names on the image. Coe spoke to people who were already organized around an issue, as opposed to simply sharing a common interest. The activists were well prepared to articulate their desires for the billboard to Coe. As a result, *Go Vegetarian* offers an unambiguous message, unlike the more evocative *daydreams &* and *Forever Champions*.

Leon Golub

SPEAK ART!

Leon Golub's billboard addresses two topics important to North Adams residents: labor unions and art. MASS MoCA is located in a 13-acre factory complex that was once world-headquarters of the Sprague Electric Company, and formerly the city's largest employer (employing one-quarter of the city's 16,000 residents). Golub met with former union leaders who vividly remember the bitter last days at "Sprague's," as local people still call the site, and the 1970 strike.

Golub's work has four elements: a purple screaming eagle diving in from the left; "SPEAK ART/ SPEAK LIBERTY" in red placed at a dynamic angle at the center top; a powerful green forearm with a clenched fist shooting up from the lower right; and the phrase "BE HEARD!" at the far right. The billboard seamlessly suggests that art, in its constant testing of the limits of free expression (to "speak art" is to "speak liberty"), represents the best qualities of America (the beautiful screaming eagle), that art's power is bound up with that of anyone who challenges the status quo (the fist, which represents labor or civil rights activism), and that all of us should aspire to "be heard!"

Although Golub's billboard could be effective in many cities, it could not be more appropriate for North Adams. This blue-collar city has had a significant role in United States' labor history for over a century, which residents are proud to share. With the closing of Sprague Electric and the subsequent opening of MASS MoCA, the character of North Adams is changing. In response, Golub succinctly presents a kinship between the traditional concerns of labor and those of art, deftly uniting the two.

AK ART
AK LIBERTY

BE
HEARD!

GOLUB

Gary Simmons

Forever Champions

All the artists MASS MoCA commissioned to make billboards were invited
to find a local group with which to work. Gary Simmons, who looked for
community partners in Adams, was overwhelmed with choices. Adams was
the birthplace of Susan B. Anthony, so there are people who work to preserve
her memory; it once had a large Quaker population, so there are people
committed to Quakerism; it is home to the largest mountain in
Massachusetts (Mount Greylock); it has an active Polish community centered
in the beautiful Saint Stanislaus Cathedral. All these facets of Adams
appealed to Simmons, but what really caught his attention was basketball.
The small town of Adams has an outstanding legacy of victory in basketball.
The teams of the late thirties, forties, and fifties were amazing, often going
to state finals to play teams from much larger cities.

Simmons met with some of the men responsible for Adams' reputation at
the Polish National Alliance, a local bar. He was regaled with stories of
their unstoppable running game, or "racehorse basketball" style, and of the
intensity of the fans' devotion. In 1956, for example, four season ticket-
holders sued the principal because they didn't get their ideal seats. A 40-year
old rumor was revisited: when the 1950 team was in Boston for the cham-
pionship, it is rumored that the coach took the seniors to a burlesque show.
"That was an artistic exhibition," one of the participants maintained, smiling.

In *Forever Champions,* four photographs of an Adams High trophy, recognizable to any graduate of the school, fill the background. In the fore-
ground, Simmons has placed the word "Champions," which is blurred – as
if it appeared there with great speed like the players on Adams' beloved
racehorse basketball team.

These billboards, made at varying times and places over the last thirty years, were recreated for the MASS MoCA exhibition and installed on major roadways in Western Massachusetts from May 30 through September 30, 1999.

Mind Control Experiments is one of ten 2' x 6' posters collectively called *Communism is Dead: Let's Fight About It* that Badger pasted on bus stop benches. As a self-affirmed agitprop (agitation propaganda) artist, Badger uses advertising venues for overtly political art that aspires both to entertain and to induce social change. *Mind Control Experiments* refers primarily to the idea of advertising itself as mind control and glancingly to actual mind control experiments or pop culture paranoid fiction (of which *The X-Files* is a recent example). Badger's bench billboard, placed innocuously on a city street, causes nearby advertisements to be regarded with heightened suspicion, encouraging viewers to search for possible hidden messages. In this context, *Mind Control Experiments* interferes with the uncritical acceptance with which most billboards are met. Badger's work on billboards, posters, and other public media aligns itself with an array of art that responds to advertising, including works by Robbie Conal, Grennen and Sperandio, and Barbara Kruger.

Peggy Diggs

PAUL
BADGER

*Mind Control
Experiments*
Columbus, Ohio
1994

Retrospective

One of seven works in a billboard exhibition sponsored by FirstBank Minneapolis and a local arts group called Film in the Cities, this image first existed as a photograph. *Artside Out* featured photographs-turned-billboards by Cindy Sherman, Barbara Kruger, William Wegman, Martha Rosler, and others and was organized by Lynne Sowder, then curator of the adventurous First Bank contemporary collection, and later organizer of a billboard project for domestic violence awareness sponsored by Liz Claiborne. The exhibition had a technical flaw that highlights the challenges of transposing fine art to a gigantically scaled medium: although all the maquettes submitted by the artists were glossy photographs, the billboards were painted by hand. The tempera paint used by the billboard painters gave all the works a matte finish. Baldessari's black and white photograph translated well, though it lost some of the film still aura it would otherwise have had. (In MASS MoCA's exhibition the work is reproduced mechanically, not hand-painted.)

In Baldessari's image, a woman and a man smile mildly at one another from opposite edges of the billboard. Superimposed on the wide expanse between them is another photograph of a fox that crawls through stormy skies on a narrow log from the woman toward the man. Whatever is communicated between them must be more ominous than the two mild faces imply. Baldessari's allegory of communication is uniquely suited to the billboard medium, which is essentially a large venue for one-way communication, and becomes meta-communicative without actually conveying anything.

Laura Steward Heon

JOHN BALDESSARI

Man and Woman with Bridge
Minneapolis, 1985

Collection Ealan Wingate, New York.

This work was part of a 1991 exhibition of billboards intended to explore "the meanings of power and communication in a democratic society... and the rights of the individual voice within the public (always already an institutional designation) realm."[1] The image (a photo-collage) focuses on a woman in a masculine pose. She maintains fierce eye-contact with the viewer, one hand on her hip and the other clenched, wearing a pink satin jacket over a Harley-Davidson t-shirt; in the background, an empty factory, an empty high chair, and scrolling stock market listings describe conditions of this woman's life. Superimposed in large type over the image is the command: SHUT DOWN FREE TRADE. The work refers to the decision by the Canadian government at that time to accept the Free Trade Agreement with the United States. The image and text express Canadian workers' fear that Canadian jobs might be lost, and that the loss would have a disastrous effect.

Conde and Beveridge have focused on the inequities of labor, gender, class and on unions throughout their years of collaboration. Like many artists who deliver social commentary with a direct, reportage-like technique (such as Loraine Leeson and Peter Dunn, Esther Parada, and Daniel Martinez), Conde and Beveridge have been overlooked by the art press for their didaticism. In public places, however, the clearly expressed populism of their messages is well-received by general audiences.

PD

1. Lianne Payne. *IN CONTROL.* Windsor, Ontario, 1991, p. 3.

KARL BEVERIDGE
AND CAROL CONDE

Shut Down
Free Trade
Windsor, Ontario
1991

Retrospective

Commissioned for the 1992 exhibition *Pour la suite du monde,* celebrating the opening of an annex to the Musée d'art contemporain de Montréal, *La Voie Lactée* was placed prominently on the roof of the new building. Cadieux's sensual image of thin red lips filling the frame has a surreal quality in its contextual isolation and dream-like luminescence. This radiance is especially apparent in the Montréal display: the photograph is lit from behind, allowing increased visibility against the night sky, in reference to the celestial body that is its namesake. Cadieux's work recalls Man Ray's painting *A l'heure de l'Observatoire- Les Amoureux,* in which a pair of red lips are pressed together and hover over a landscape in a cloudy evening sky. Had the technology of the day permitted, Man Ray would have photographically reproduced the image in the grand dimensions he desired, as Cadieux has done.[1]

Representative of Cadieux's oeuvre, which often deals with extreme close-ups of the body, *La Voie Lactée* is one of two billboards created by the artist over the last 12 years. This work, like Felix Gonzalez-Torres' *Untitled (Bed)* or John Baldessari's *Man and Woman with a Bridge,* uses the billboard format to juxtapose intimacy and grand scale with great effect.

Lisa Dorin

1. Man Ray wrote: "If there had been a color process enabling me to make a photograph of such dimensions [39 3/8'x 98'] and showing the lips floating over a landscape, I would certainly have preferred to do it that way." Man Ray, *Man Ray: Self Portrait.* Boston/Toronto: Little, Brown & Company, 1963, p. 253.

GENEVIÈVE CADIEUX

La Voie Lactée (the Milky Way)
Montreal, 1992

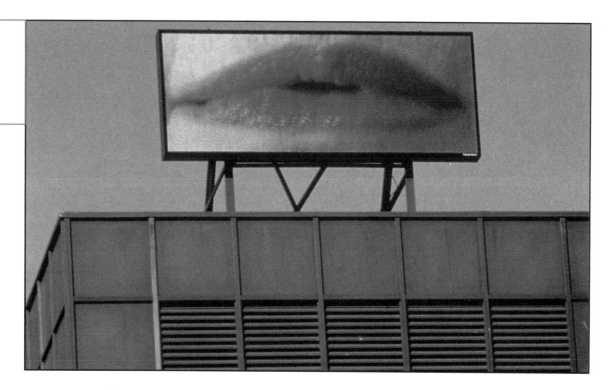

Made in collaboration with Graphicstudio / USF, a print workshop affiliated with the University of South Florida in Tampa, *A Single Screw of Flesh* is one of four billboards in a suite Dill designed featuring excerpts from poems by Emily Dickinson and enigmatic photographs of friends. These are unusual billboards for technical reasons: printed on large sheets of vinyl that Graphicstudio will keep, they are unique, permanent objects (unlike most billboards, which are destroyed) that could be installed on any 14' x 48' billboard structure. The works are the first products of Graphicstudio's Public Editions program, whose goal is to bring high-quality graphic art to the general public.

A Single Screw of Flesh ("A Single Screw of Flesh -/ is All that Pins the Soul-") is a typically Dickinsonian couplet in its sparseness, evocativeness, and precision. In her billboard, Dill combines this line with a photograph of a man, hand on chin in a melancholy pose, whose body is covered with the text of the poem. The lines of text encircle his body like the threads of Dickinson's screw. In this billboard, as in Geneviève Cadieux's *La Voie Lactèe* or Felix Gonzalez-Torres's *Untitled (Bed)*, Dill successfully marries a delicate sentiment and a gross format through the compact strength of her design.   LSH

LESLEY DILL

A Single Screw of Flesh
Tampa, Florida
1998

Retrospective

Lesley Dill : Artist   Emily Dickinson : Poet   Graphicstudio/*USF* : Publisher   Steve Carlisle : Digital

Commissioned by the Museum of Modern Art for the *Projects* series of younger artists, Gonzalez-Torres's black and white photograph of an empty bed appeared at 24 locations in Manhattan for a month-long exhibition in the summer of 1992. The only billboard MoMA has commissioned, the work exists today as a 4" x 5" color transparency in the museum's permanent collection, making it one of a handful that is owned by an institution.

This ghostly image of a warm and inviting bed, its blanket turned down, is one of the most subtle billboards dealing with AIDS among the relatively large number of billboards addressing the issue. The work is a tribute to Gonzalez-Torres's lover, who died of the virus. The empty bed is a poignant marker of the loss of a life partner, the person who shared the bed. The placement of such an intimate image as a bed on the streets of New York is also a telling comment on privacy issues surrounding the HIV/AIDS epidemic: the disease forces the legacy of intimate acts to be made public.

Felix Gonzalez-Torres was a prolific billboard maker both individually and as a member of the collectives Gran Fury and Group Material. Many of his billboards attacked AIDS issues; indeed, the subtle expressiveness of *Untitled (Bed)* stands in sharp contrast to the explicit directives in his other works. The use of the blunt instrument of a billboard to convey such a delicate and tragic intimacy secured this work's place in the MASS MoCA exhibition.   LSH

**FELIX
GONZALEZ-TORRES**
Untitled (Bed)
New York, 1992

The Museum of Modern Art, New York,
Gift of Werner and Elaine Dannheisser

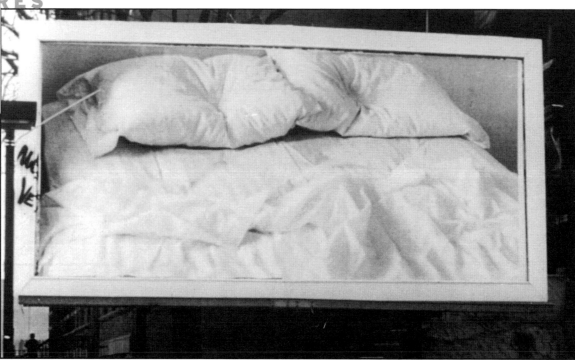

The collective Gran Fury was formed in 1988 by artists and designers working with the AIDS Coalition to Unleash Power (ACT UP) and was largely responsible for ACT UP's potent propaganda machine. Gran Fury's media were crack-and-peel stickers, t-shirts, placards, posters, and billboards, and their sly appropriation of advertising styles suited these media perfectly. The timeliness of their art attacks, the vociferous presentation of hard facts about AIDS, and the sophistication of their designs make them among the most important billboard-makers of the last thirty years. The majority of Gran Fury's graphics are concerned with AIDS and were made from 1988 to 1992, when President Ronald Reagan and New York's mayor Edward Koch were downplaying the mushrooming health crisis. Although HIV/AIDS remains one of the most pressing issues of our time, Gran Fury's AIDS billboards of the late 1980s and early 1990s, which were so effective in New York City at that time, would be received with some puzzlement in the Berkshires in 1999. *Welcome to America* (the whole text reads: "Welcome to America/ the only industrialized nation besides South Africa without national health care") represents Gran Fury's work in this exhibition. This billboard, like the AIDS works, made its strongest point in 1989 when South Africa was in the last days of apartheid, but nonetheless its message endures and applies equally well in rural Massachusetts and urban New York. The upper text, "Welcome to America," is separated from the punchline printed along the bottom by a plump brown-eyed baby. The tragic implication is that this American baby would receive the same poor quality of health care whether in the United States or apartheid-stricken South Africa. LSH

GRAN FURY
Welcome to America
New York, 1989

Retrospective

We May Not Have Homes was one of several billboards in the *Your Message Here project*, organized jointly by Group Material and the Randolf Street Gallery in Chicago. The artists' collective Group Material collaborated with individuals and activist groups in Chicago to design billboards for their neighborhoods. For the billboard *Ningun Humano es Ilegal* (No Human is Illegal), for example, Group Material worked with the Catholic Parishoners of Pilsen; *Talk About It* was made with the Chicago branch of the AIDS Coalition to Unleash Power (ACT UP); *This will not be our birth control,* with photographs of coat hangers, was made with Sister Serpents.

The Chicago/Gary Union of the Homeless made *We May Not Have Homes* ("We May Not Have Homes/ But We Do Have Names/ And We Live Here Too"). This billboard, covered by the signatures of the homeless, was installed in a neighborhood where many homeless people live. This restrained and dignified text makes a simple plea for recognition. The poignant statement "we do have names" insists that these homeless people be acknowledged as individuals, and the line "we live here too" proclaims their status as neighbors and citizens.   LSH

GROUP MATERIAL + RANDOLPH STREET GALLERY

The Chicago/Gary
Union of the
Homeless

*We May Not
Have Homes*
Chicago, 1990

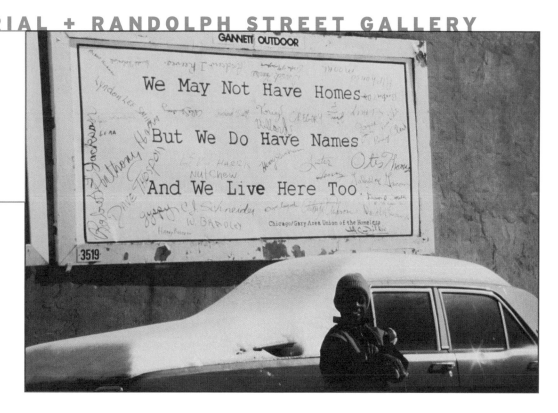

Commissioned by the Public Art Fund, which supports public art projects in greater New York City, *Met. Museum* was never produced as a billboard until MASS MoCA did so for this exhibition. The billboard company found the shape of the fan held by the odalisque wearing a gorilla mask (the hallmark of the Guerrilla Girls) to be phallic and declined to install the work. The nudity of the odalisque, however, raised no objections, which is ironic, given the text of the billboard: "Do women have to be naked to get into the Met. Museum? Less than 5% of the artists in the Modern Art Sections are women, but 85% of the nudes are female." The Guerrilla Girls produced another billboard, commenting vociferously on the censoring of the first, which was installed instead. The unproduced work gained notoriety, however. The Guerrilla Girls are an anonymous, sometimes vigilante organization that bills itself as the conscience of the art world in matters of gender inequality. The Girls are one of several important collectives, such as Gran Fury and Group Material, that were formed in the 1980s. These groups made billboards, bus posters, hand bills, bumper stickers, and other ephemera that was distributed widely in New York. Their subjects were the social tragedies of the day (many of which remain tragic today): domestic abuse, health care inequity, homelessness, AIDS, drug abuse, and gender inequity.   LSH

* The Guerilla Girls made one change in the MASS MoCA version: they removed the word "Met" from the first line, making the image more universal. Refer to page 19 for the original image.

GUERRILLA GIRLS

Met. Museum
New York, 1988

Retrospective

Do women have to be naked to get into art museums?

Less than 5% of the artists in NY's Metropolitan Museum are women, but 85% of the nudes are female.*

* In the Modern and Contemporary art sections

A PUBLIC SERVICE MESSAGE FROM **GUERRILLA GIRLS** CONSCIENCE OF THE ART WORLD
www.guerrillagirls.com

Keith Haring's bold graphic style lent itself easily to the billboard format: it is inventive and lively, but legible at any scale. This powerful image depicting the dangers of crack, communicated through stylized, thick, black lines, is easily recognizable as a Haring design. From a small, partially visible crack pipe in the lower left corner billows a vast puff of smoke with a didactic yet colloquial message: "Crack is Wack." Surrounding the cloud, around the perimeter of the image, float symbols of the inevitable destruction awaiting crack users: money going up in flames, followed by two ghostly skulls and human figures subjected to various tortures by razor-toothed monsters.

As an unorthodox but wildly popular public artist, Haring helped shape our views towards, and inspired other artists to explore, the world of public art. Haring's work blurs the line between officially commissioned billboards and 'guerrilla' postings and graffiti art, making a retrospective of this nature a difficult task.

LD

KEITH HARING

Crack Is Wack

New York, 1985

Keith Haring Estate

Commissioned by the Wexner Center for the Arts of the Ohio State University, *Indigenous* was one of several works by native peoples in *Will/Power*, an exhibition investigating the issue of cultural identity in relation to the 500th anniversary of the arrival of Christopher Columbus in America. During the 1990s, Heap of Birds undertook several projects in which he coupled under-represented socio-political concerns of native peoples with a cool authoritarian format: large, anonymous signs and capitalized, sans-serif texts. The juxtaposition of typically straightforward tools of communication (usually used to convey simple facts or directions) with politicized messages leads the viewer to question the political structures these formats may always reflect or propagate.

The political content of Heap of Birds' billboards consistently draws on native issues, but changes in mood from mystic and poetic (as in *Sixteen Songs* installed in Dallas in 1995, which reads "SKY/ EARTH/ OFFERING/ PATIENCE") to black humor (seen in *American Leagues*, showing the smiling mascot of the Cleveland Indians baseball team and the text "SMILE FOR RACISM," installed in Cleveland in 1996, page 90). In *Indigenous* ("PRE-COLUMBIAN/ PRE-HISPANIC/ PRE-AMERICAN/ OUR NATIVE SPIRITS/ INDIGENOUS"), Heap of Birds forces us to remember that the history of this continent did not begin with the arrival of Columbus in 1492.   LSH

HACHIVI EDGAR
HEAP OF BIRDS

Indigenous
Columbus, Ohio
1992

Retrospective

Jenny Holzer has used language both as content and image since her early series of *Truisms* in the late 1970s. Her private verities range from small posters to billboards, metal signs, stickers, LED lights, or carved stone. Varied typefaces, a range of lengths of messages, colored grounds, colored lights and distinct surfaces differentiate the works, as do their mobile or static presentation. With each series the 'voice' of the message changes as well, some seeming to represent a variety of regular people with differing biases, others from inflammatory extremists. Holzer works both within interior art venues where she can control the installation and present lengthy scrolling texts, and outdoors where her text is succinct and more easily consumable. In her public work, she often subverts dispassionate sites of information by introducing a level of complexity and ambiguity usually experienced in private spaces.

The billboard exhibited by MASS MoCA is from her *Survival* series of texts, which was exhibited in multiple public and private sites across the United States in the mid-1980s. The work argues for survival through sustaining imagination, but its fragile optimism implies a nonetheless hopeless existence.

PD

JENNY HOLZER
Untitled
(OUTER SPACE)
New York, 1984

Class 4, Matter, I. Matter in General, the first artist's billboard in the United States, was enigmatic when it was installed in the New Mexico desert in 1968 and remains so today. Kosuth listed seven apparently random elements of matter on the billboard, beginning with "universe" and ending with "resins". The roman numeral I. at the heading and the numbers 374 – 380 imply that this list is excerpted from a larger one. (In fact, the text is excerpted from *Roget's Thesaurus.*) The text on the billboard is part of Kosuth's *The Second Investigation,* a group of documents and plans now in the collection of the Van Abbemuseum. Other texts from *The Second Investigation* were exhibited on at least three billboards in addition to this one: *Class 3, Physics, II. Heat,* in Turin, *Class 3, Physics, IV. Electricity and Electronics,* in Pasadena, CA, and *Class 5, Sensation, IV. Smell,* shown in Bern, Switzerland, all in 1969. The texts can also appear as photostats mounted on gallery walls and in newspapers and magazines. Unlike the majority of artists' billboards, *The Second Investigation* makes no overt political statement, nor does it offer visual interest. In 1969, Kosuth wrote that his choice of ephemeral public media grew from a desire to stress the immateriality of the work and to sever any connection with painting. "The new work is not connected with a precious object – it's accessible to as many people as are interested."[1] Interestingly, although this is the oldest work in the exhibition, *Class 4, Matter, I. Matter in General* retains its radical quality better than the majority of billboards made later, whose styles have been assimilated into the dominant visual culture.   LSH

1. Joseph Kosuth. *January 5-31, 1969.* Exhibition Catalogue. New York: Seth Siegelaub, 1969, n.p.

JOSEPH KOSUTH

Class 4, Matter 1. Matter in General
Albuquerque, New Mexico, 1968

Retrospective

Commissioned by the Portland Museum of Art in 1992, Kruger's potent image appeared on billboards and buses throughout the city. The text speaks to the highly political atmosphere that surrounded the narrow defeat of the statewide anti-gay ballot initiative at the time of the exhibition. The phrase "Do to others as you would have them do to you," which appeared in the corners of the Portland version, directly addressed the issues of prejudice and discrimination that dominated the discourse at the time.

Intently deflecting our gaze, a generic middle-aged man turns his head away from us in extreme profile. A text block stamped across his face and padlocked door hinged to his head further distance the subject from the viewer. The lock and the confrontational phrase, "Fear and hate make you small, bitter, and mean," unequivocally state the artist's attitude toward intolerance.

Barbara Kruger's work has had a profound impact on the history of artists' billboards. Adroitly unifying popular advertising techniques, elements of high modernist and experimental photography, and politically charged slogans, her images exemplify the spirit of the public art medium.

LD

BARBARA KRUGER
Fear and Hate
Portland, Oregon
1992

Les Levine has arguably worked longer in the public arena than other artists chronicled here, utilizing technology and public sites since the mid-1960s to make what he calls "disposable art." He focuses on finding a relationship between image and text that is generally and vaguely loaded, so that viewers can find a self-relevant logic and meaning for themselves in his work. These two billboards were from an early outdoor billboard campaign of five billboards called *AIM, RACE, TAKE, STEAL*, and *FORGET*, which were shown both sequentially along a highway and randomly in the city. In this series, he presented directive verbs (aim, race, take, steal, and forget) and corresponding images (a deer, horse, mechanical crane, building, and a herd of elephants, respectively). These were "devised to elicit a flurry of internal meanings based on the rebus (race-horse), the pun (steal-steel), folkloric associations (elephants-forgetting) or mental associations of nature being acted upon by man (deer-aim, earth-machine.)"[1] In *TAKE* and *AIM*, Levine uses reductive images, flat planes of bright colors, single, mostly monosyllabic words, and a medium (the billboard) not known for its subtlety to create evocative, nuanced works of art.   PD

1. Dominique Nahas. *Public Mind: Les Levin's Media Sculpture and Mass Ad Campaigns 1969-1990.* Everson, Illinois: Everson Museum of Art, 1990, p. 26.

LES LEVINE
Take, Aim
Minneapolis, 1983

Retrospective

Pratt's colorful mackerel was commissioned for *Painting the Town,* an exhibition of hand-painted billboards sponsored by the Manufacturers Life Insurance Company in 1987, which toured nine Canadian cities. This straightforward but lively image of a blue mackerel on a bright red, pink, and turquoise background is striking in such a large format. Interestingly, *Painting the Town* was one of several billboard exhibitions throughout Canada; there have been billboard exhibitions in Saskatoon, Saskatchewan *(The Post-colonial Landscape)* in 1993, Burlington, Ontario (*Reading the Water*) in 1992, and Regina, Saskatchewan (*Regina Billboard Project*) in 1989-90, among others. Because of its large format, temporality, and accessibility to the public, the billboard serves as the perfect vehicle for local artists to gain recognition and have their work more widely viewed than perhaps otherwise possible. Locally sponsored exhibitions have been the source for many of the billboards included in the survey.   LD

MARY PRATT
Decked Mackerel
(Big Mac)
Toronto, 1987

Kay Rosen arranges letters the way a Dutch baroque painter might arrange elements in a still life. She sets narrow alphabetic parameters for herself in each text-based piece, as a painter might with a bowl of fruit, and makes the most of what she finds there, often with considerable wit. Several artists in BILLBOARD work exclusively with text (Jenny Holzer and Joseph Kosuth, for example), but none focuses primarily on letters rather than words. A former linguistics student, Rosen investigates language at the level of the letter.

In *Hi*, Rosen lists the letters of the alphabet from A to I, presenting the last two letters, H and I, in a different color than the others in the list. By this simple designation in the series of the word "hi," which is a homonym of the word "high," she has visually and semantically isolated the 'high' end of the series. The presentation of the greeting "hi" on a billboard, in addition to the wordplay set up by the title, links Rosen's work to the meta-communicative works of John Baldessari and Geneviève Cadieux.

LSH

KAY ROSEN

Hi

Lewisburg, Pennsylvania

1997

Retrospective

The political resonance of Erika Rothenberg's *Traditional Families* is clear from a quick glance at the billboard. A blue-eyed nuclear family (complete with blue-eyed dog) and clean, light-colored blocky text are arranged simply on a dark background. The smiling family is a version of reality often touted by conservative political groups, and the banality and conservatism of the image sets up the surprising irony of Rothenberg's punch-line: "4%." By coupling this plain, cheery design with the surprising statistic that only 4% of American families are traditional (working father, housewife, two children), Rothenberg suggests that we question the reality of the advertising images presented to us daily.

Her billboard *Teenagers Don't Die of AIDS* functions in a similar way: the title text is separated from the ironic punch line ("It's usually a time bomb that goes off in your 20's. USE A CONDOM") by a graphically restrained image of smiling teenagers (page 99). Gran Fury's *Welcome to America* packs a comparable ironic punch by combining a cheery slogan and photograph of a plump baby with the grim truth of health care availability in the United States (page 55).   LSH

ERIKA ROTHENBERG
Traditional Families
Los Angeles
1990

4

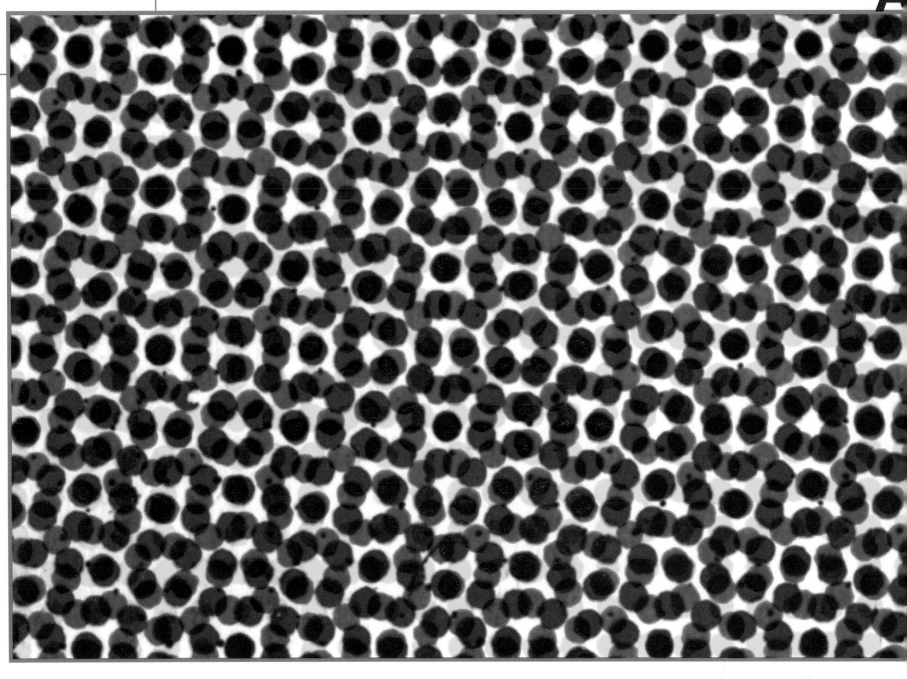

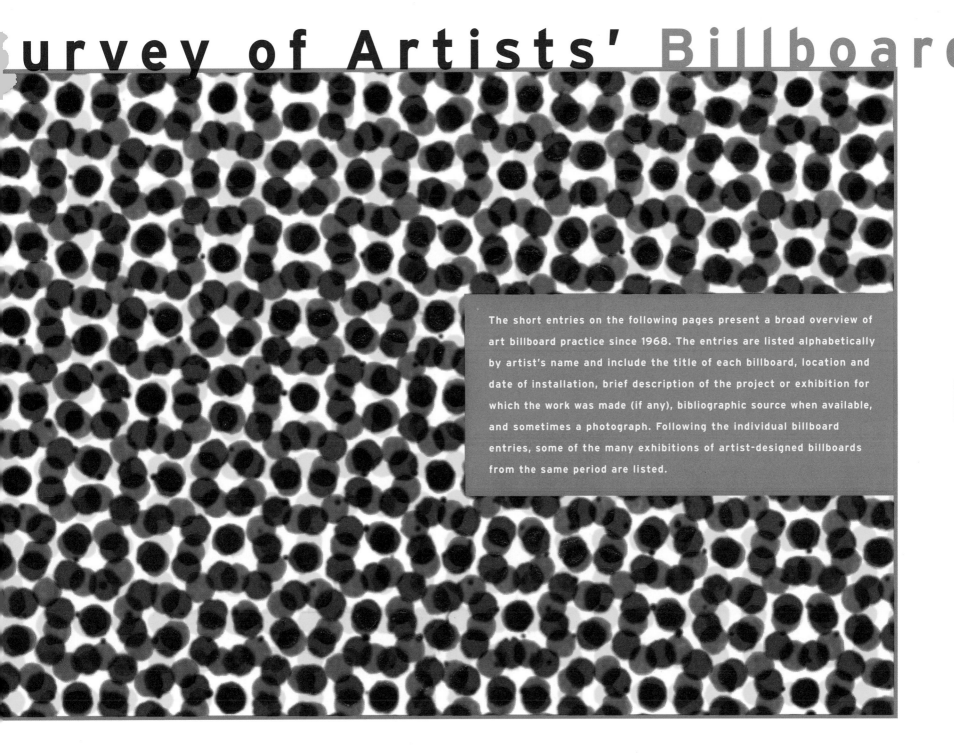

The short entries on the following pages present a broad overview of
art billboard practice since 1968. The entries are listed alphabetically
by artist's name and include the title of each billboard, location and
date of installation, brief description of the project or exhibition for
which the work was made (if any), bibliographic source when available,
and sometimes a photograph. Following the individual billboard
entries, some of the many exhibitions of artist-designed billboards
from the same period are listed.

DENNIS ADAMS
Bus Shelter I
New York, 1983-87
Project: Collaboration
with Jenny Holzer.
Source: Dennis Adams. *Dennis Adams:*
Architecture of Amnesia.
With an essay by Mary-Anne Staniszweski.
New York: Kent Fine Art, 1990.

WILLIAM ANASTASI
Læser En Linje På Et Skilt
(Reading a line on a billboard) Location unknown,
1967 (per the artist); Copenhagen, 1991
Project: *Projekt Gadetegn,* an exhibition featuring the
work of 112 artists on 117 billboards in Copenhagen.
Source: Biz Art. *Projekt Gadetegn.*
Copenhagen: Biz Art, 1991.

DENNIS ADAMS
Fallen Angels
Graz, Austria, 1988
Project: *Points of Reference* 1938/1988,
an exhibition of temporary public installations on sites of
Nazi indoctrination in Austria.
Source: Dennis Adams. *Dennis Adams: Architecture of Amnesia.*
With an essay by Mary-Anne Staniszweski.
New York: Kent Fine Art, 1990.

RASHEED ARAEEN
The Golden Verses
London, 1990-91
Project: Sponsored by the Artangel Trust,
multiple billboards of this image were installed in London.
Source: Guy Brett. "Rasheed Araeen." *Art in America,*
March 1991.

Survey

DENNIS ADAMS
Kunstinsel
Hamburg, 1989
Project: *D & S Ausstellung,* an international exhibition sponsored by
Hamburg Kunstverein in public sites and
buildings scheduled for demolition.
Source: Dennis Adams. *Dennis Adams: Architecture of Amnesia.*
With an essay by Mary-Anne Staniszweski.
New York: Kent Fine Art, 1990.

BARBARA ASTMAN
Untitled
Calgary, 1988
Project: *Art on Billboards,* sponsored by the
Calgary Olympic Arts Festival for the 1988
Winter Olympics.
Source: Hamilton, Ontario, Art Gallery of
Hamilton, *Barbara Astman: Personal/Persona:*
A 20-Year Survey, 1995.

DENNIS ADAMS
Pedestrian Tunnels
Esslingen, Germany, 1989
Project: *International Foto-Triennale.*
Source: Dennis Adams. *Dennis Adams: Architecture of Amnesia.*
With an essay by Mary-Anne Staniszweski.
New York: Kent Fine Art, 1990.

PAUL BADGER
Communism is Dead: Let's Fight About it
Columbus, Ohio, 1994
Project: *Communism is Dead: Let's Fight About It,*
a master's thesis project with 10 bench billboards.
Source: The artist.

PAUL BADGER

Take Down the House with the Master's Tools
Columbus, Ohio, 1994
Project: *Communism is Dead: Let's Fight About It,*
a master's thesis project with 10 bench billboards.
Source: The artist.

PAUL BADGER

Women Have Always Worked
Columbus, Ohio, 1994
Project: *Communism is Dead: Let's Fight About It,*
a master's thesis project with 10 bench billboards.
Source: The artist.

PAUL BADGER

Prisons and Police – America's Growth Industries
Columbus, Ohio, 1994
Project: *Communism is Dead: Let's Fight About It,*
a master's thesis project with 10 bench billboards.
Source: The artist.

PAUL BADGER

Dreams Begin and End in Reality
Columbus, Ohio, 1994
Project: *Communism is Dead: Let's Fight About It,*
a master's thesis project with 10 bench billboards.
Source: The artist.

PAUL BADGER

Mind Control Experiments – Next 5 Miles
Columbus, Ohio, 1994
Project: *Communism is Dead: Let's Fight About It,*
a master's thesis project with 10 bench billboards.
Source: The artist.

PAUL BADGER

Inner Joy – Stop the Itch, Heal the Rash
Columbus, Ohio, 1994
Project: *Communism is Dead: Let's Fight About It,*
a master's thesis project with 10 bench billboards.
Source: The artist.

PAUL BADGER

Guns Keep Us Apart
Columbus, Ohio, 1994
Project: *Communism is Dead: Let's Fight About It,*
a master's thesis project with 10 bench billboards.
Source: The artist.

PAUL BADGER

55977ing
Columbus, Ohio, 1994
Project: *Communism is Dead: Let's Fight About It,*
a master's thesis project with 10 bench billboards.
Source: The artist.

JOHN BALDESSARI
Man and Woman with Bridge
Minneapolis, 1985
Project: *Artside Out,* an exhibition of
8 photographs by 8 artists on billboards.
Source: Minneapolis, Film in the Cities, First Banks,
Artside Out, 1985.

RON BENNER
Native to the Americas
Windsor, Ontario, 1991
Project: *In Control,* an exhibition of six billboards
organized by Artcite Gallery.
Source: Windsor, Ontario, Artcite Gallery,
In Control, 1991.

JOHN BALDESSARI
*Untitled (Speech is Silver,
Silence is Golden, Action is $)*
Multiple locations, 1989
Project: *Art Against AIDS/On the Road,* to benefit the American
Foundation for AIDS Research; billboards shown in San Francisco,
Washington, DC, and Chicago throughout 1989 and 1990.
Source: Kristen Engberg. "Marketing the Adjusted Cause."
New Art Examiner, May 1991.

BILLBOARD LIBERATION FRONT
Project: Anonymous guerilla group that has been
"liberating" billboards for the last twenty years in the
Los Angeles area.

Survey

BEN BAKER
Peaches at Sunset
Alabama, 1994
Project: *Alabama Artists Outdoor,* sponsored by the Alabama State
Council on the Arts to promote the work of Alabama artists.
Source: Kathy Holland. "Taking Art to the Streets: The Alabama
Artists Outdoor Project." *Alabama Arts.* Montgomery: Alabama State
Council on the Arts, Spring 1994, pp. 13-15.

JEAN-CHARLES BLAIS
Untitled (National Assembly of France)
Paris, 1990
Project: An installation in the Assemblée Nationale metro
station redone every month for upkeep until 2000.
Source: Deborah Wye. *Thinking Print: Books to Billboa*
1980-95. New York: Museum of Modern Art, distributed
Harry Abrams, 1996, pp. 16, 25.

ALAN BELCHER
Kill Me
Suburban Copenhagen, 1992; Toronto, 1997
Project: (1992 version) *Paradise Europe,* an exhibition of 120
billboards of work by 13 artists; (1997 version) sponsored by and
displayed in the Art Metropole Gallery as part of
Billboards by Artists Series.
Source: Copenhagen, Biz Art, *Paradise Europe,* 1992.

JOHN BOONE
Resort Development
Brooklyn, New York, 1982
Project: Simulated construction company
announcement in the Gowanus Canal.
Source: The artist.

KATHRYN BRACKETT-LUCH
Untitled
Ferndale, Michigan, 1998
Project: Installation in billboard space at
Revolution Gallery in Ferndale, Michigan,
in suburban Detroit.
Source: Revolution Gallery.

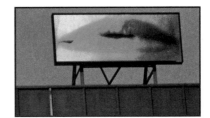

GENEVIÈVE CADIEUX
Nature Morte aux Arbres et au Ballon
(Still Life with Trees and Ball)
Montréal, 1987 and 1991
Project: Designed for the exhibition *Elementae Natura,*
organized by the Musée d'art contemporain de Montréal
in 1987; shown again in *Crossroads* exhibition at
The Art Gallery of York University in Toronto in 1991.
Source: Musée d'art contemporain de Montréal.

RICHARD BROUGH
Jones Street at Noon
Tuscaloosa, Alabama, 1994
Project: *Alabama Artists Outdoor,* sponsored by the Alabama
State Council on the Arts to promote the work of Alabama artists.
Source: Kathy Holland. "'Taking Art to the Streets'":
The Alabama Artists Outdoor Project." *Alabama Arts.*
Montgomery: Alabama State Council on the Arts,
Spring 1994, pp. 13-15.

GENEVIÈVE CADIEUX
La Voie Lactée (The Milky Way)
Montréal, 1992
Project: Designed for the exhibition *Pour la Suite
du Monde,* organized by the Musée d'Art
Contemporain de Montréal in 1992.
Source: Musée d'art contemporain de Montréal.

CHRISTINE BURCHNALL
Improving Your View of the World ...
Windsor, Ontario, 1991
Project: *In Control,* an exhibition of six
billboards organized by Artcite Gallery.
Source: Windsor, Ontario, Artcite Gallery,
In Control, 1991.

**JEANINE CENTOURI and
RUSSELL ROCK**
Scopes
Ferndale, Michigan, 1998
Project: Collaborative piece installed in billboard
space at Revolution Gallery in Ferndale,
Michigan, in suburban Detroit.
Source: Revolution Gallery.

CARYL BURTNER
Look Before You Leap
Richmond, Virginia, 1986
Project: Individual billboard project.
Source: The artist.

CLASS ACTION
Untitled (He hits me, he hits me not)
New Haven, Connecticut, 1995
Project: Collective work installed in conjunction
with domestic violence awareness campaign.
Source: Class Action: The Art Collective for
Community Action, 212 York Street,
New Haven CT 06520.

**CAROL CONDE AND
KARL BEVERIDGE**

Shut Down Free Trade

Windsor, Ontario, 1991

Project: *In Control,* an exhibition of six billboards
organized by Artcite Gallery.

Source: Windsor, Ontario, Artcite Gallery,
In Control, 1991.

MARK COOPER

Untitled (Against Violence)

Washington, DC, 1995

Project: Collaborative project with hundreds of
young people over several years
in Boston and Washington, DC.

Source: The artist.

MARK COOPER

Untitled (Nonviolence '94)

Washington, DC, 1995

Project: Collaborative project with hundreds of
young people over several years
in Boston and Washington, DC.

Source: The artist.

MARK COOPER

Untitled (Stop the Violence)

Washington, DC, 1995

Project: Collaborative project with hundreds
of young people over several years
in Boston and Washington, DC.

Source: The artist.

Survey

MARK COOPER

Untitled (Against Violence)

Washington, DC, 1995

Project: Collaborative project with hundreds of
young people over several years
in Boston and Washington, DC.

Source: The artist.

MARK COOPER

Untitled (Get Along Together)

Boston, 1996

Project: Collaborative project with hundreds
of young people over several years
in Boston and Washington, DC.

Source: The artist.

MARK COOPER

Untitled (Nonviolence '94)

Washington, DC, 1995

Project: Collaborative project with hundreds of
young people over several years
in Boston and Washington, DC.

Source: The artist.

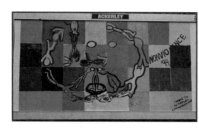

MARK COOPER

Untitled (Please)

Boston, 1996

Project: Collaborative project with hundreds of
young people over several years in Boston and
Washington, DC.

Source: The artist.

MARK COOPER
Untitled
Boston, 1996
Project: Collaborative project with hundreds
of young people over several years in Boston
and Washington, DC.
Source: The artist.

MARK COOPER
Untitled (Say No Violence)
Boston, 1997
Project: Collaborative project with hundreds
of young people over several years
in Boston and Washington, DC.
Source: The artist.

MARK COOPER
Untitled (No __ Violence)
Boston, 1996
Project: Collaborative project with hundreds
of young people over several years
in Boston and Washington, DC.
Source: The artist.

MARK COOPER
Untitled (Violence Makes Me Sick)
Boston, 1997
Project: Collaborative project with hundreds
of young people over several years
in Boston and Washington, DC.
Source: The artist.

MARK COOPER
Untitled (Flag)
Boston, 1996
Project: Collaborative project with hundreds of
young people over several years
in Boston and Washington, DC.
Source: The artist.

MARK COOPER
Untitled
Boston, 1997
Project: Collaborative project with hundreds
of young people over several years in Boston
and Washington, DC.
Source: The artist.

MARK COOPER
Untitled (No Violence)
Boston, 1996
Project: Collaborative project with hundreds of
young people over several years
in Boston and Washington, DC.
Source: The artist.

MARK COOPER
Untitled (Art Against Violence)
Boston, 1997
Project: Collaborative project with hundreds
of young people over several years
in Boston and Washington, DC.
Source: The artist.

CULTURE INDUSTRIES
Seditious Sound Bite
Ferndale, Michigan, 1997
Project: Installed in billboard space at Revolution Gallery in Ferndale, Michigan, in suburban Detroit.
Source: Revolution Gallery.

PEGGY DIGGS,
with DocentTeens at the Institute of Contemporary Art, Boston
Here Are Ours
Boston, 1995
Project: HomeFront, a project in which the teen docents at the ICA addressed the importance of role models in their lives. Subway station billboard.
Source: The artist.

STEVE CURRIE
Untitled
Ferndale, Michigan, 1998
Project: Installed in billboard space at Revolution Gallery in Ferndale, Michigan, in suburban Detroit.
Source: Revolution Gallery.

PEGGY DIGGS
Domestic Violence Billboard
Lee, Adams, and Pittsfield, Massachusetts, 1991
Project: Individual billboard project.
Source: The artist.

Survey

SIMON CUTHBERT
Boral Plant
Sydney, Australia, 1997
Project: Camellia Enhancement billboard project.
Source: The artist.

PEGGY DIGGS,
with students at Hoosac Valley High School,
Adams, Massachusetts
It Would Help
Adams and Cheshire, Massachusetts, 1993
Project: Part of the Lila Wallace Reader's Digest International Artists' Grant, Home Portion.
Source: The artist.

ROSE DESLOOVER
Summer Rose
Ferndale, Michigan, 1997
Project: Installed in billboard space at Revolution Gallery in Ferndale, Michigan, in suburban Detroit.
Source: Revolution Gallery.

MATT DILLING
Money Governs Power
Washington, DC, 1996
Project: "Guerilla" billboard in response to the arrests of federal agents accused of espionage.
Source: The artist.

MATT DILLING
Nine Out of Ten People
Washington, DC, 1996
Project: "Guerilla" billboard making
a statement about belief systems.
Source: The artist.

RON ENGLISH
The New World Order
New York, 1990
Project: Part of an ongoing "guerilla" billboard
campaign beginning in 1982 in which works of
social satire are made to resemble real
commercial billboards.
Source: http://www.graffiti.org

NANCY DWYER
Obsession Overruled
Location unknown, 1985
Project: Individual billboard project.
Source: Cristinerose Gallery, New York.

RON ENGLISH
Censorship is Good Because
New York, 1990
Project: Part of an ongoing "guerilla" billboard
campaign beginning in 1982 in which works of
social satire are made to resemble real
commercial billboards.
Source: http://www.graffiti.org

OLAFUR ELIASSON
Expectation
Suburban Copenhagen, 1992
Project: *Paradise Europe,* an exhibition of 120
billboards by 13 artists.
Source: Copenhagen, Biz Art,
Paradise Europe, 1992.

RON ENGLISH
Some Freds are Gonna Roll
New York, 1990
Project: Part of an ongoing "guerilla" billboard
campaign beginning in 1982 in which works of
social satire are made to resemble real
commercial billboards.
Source: http://www.graffiti.org

ELMGREEN & OLESEN
Two Left Ears
Suburban Copenhagen, 1992
Project: *Paradise Europe,* an exhibition of
120 billboards by 13 artists.
Source: Copenhagen, Biz Art,
Paradise Europe, 1992.

RON ENGLISH
Untitled
New York, 1990
Project: Part of an ongoing "guerilla" billboard
campaign beginning in 1982 in which works of
social satire are made to resemble real
commercial billboards.
Source: http://www.graffiti.org

RON ENGLISH
Camel Jr's
New York, 1990
Project: Part of an ongoing "guerilla" billboard campaign beginning in 1982 in which works of social satire are made to resemble real commercial billboards.
Source: http://www.graffiti.org

RON ENGLISH
Cancer Kid
Jersey City, New Jersey, 1995
Project: Part of an ongoing "guerilla" billboard campaign beginning in 1982 in which works of social satire are made to resemble real commercial billboards.
Source: http://www.graffiti.org

RON ENGLISH
Cancer Kids
Jersey City, New Jersey, 1992
Project: Part of an ongoing "guerilla" billboard campaign beginning in 1982 in which works of social satire are made to resemble real commercial billboards.
Source: http://www.graffiti.org

RON ENGLISH
Liberty's First Casualty
New York, 1995
Project: Part of an ongoing "guerilla" billboard campaign beginning in 1982 in which works of social satire are made to resemble real commercial billboards.
Source: http://www.graffiti.org

Survey

RON ENGLISH
Smooth Character
Jersey City, New Jersey, 1994
Project: Part of an ongoing "guerilla" billboard campaign beginning in 1982 in which works of social satire are made to resemble real commercial billboards.
Source: http://www.graffiti.org

RON ENGLISH
Exxtinct
New York, 1995
Project: Part of an ongoing "guerilla" billboard campaign beginning in 1982 in which works of social satire are made to resemble real commercial billboards.
Source: http://www.graffiti.org

RON ENGLISH
Jesus Christ
Austin, Texas, 1994
Project: Part of an ongoing "guerilla" billboard campaign beginning in 1982 in which works of social satire are made to resemble real commercial billboards.
Source: http://www.graffiti.org

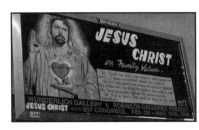

RON ENGLISH
Forever Kool
Jersey City, New Jersey, 1996
Project: Part of an ongoing "guerilla" billboard campaign beginning in 1982 in which works of social satire are made to resemble real commercial billboards.
Source: http://www.graffiti.org

RON ENGLISH
Evolve
New York, 1996
Project: Part of an ongoing "guerilla" billboard campaign beginning in 1982 in which works of social satire are made to resemble real commercial billboards.
Source: http://www.graffiti.org

RON ENGLISH
Your Apathy is Our Strength
New York, 1997
Project: Part of an ongoing "guerilla" billboard campaign beginning in 1982 in which works of social satire are made to resemble real commercial billboards.
Source: http://www.graffiti.org

RON ENGLISH
Billboard Liberation, Just Do It
Jersey City, New Jersey, 1997
Project: Part of an ongoing "guerilla" billboard campaign beginning in 1982 in which works of social satire are made to resemble real commercial billboards.
Source: http://www.graffiti.org

RON ENGLISH
Keep Hope a Lie
New York, 1997
Project: Part of an ongoing "guerilla" billboard campaign beginning in 1982 in which works of social satire are made to resemble real commercial billboards.
Source: http://www.graffiti.org

RON ENGLISH
POPaganda
Jersey City, New Jersey, 1997
Project: Part of an ongoing "guerilla" billboard campaign beginning in 1982 in which works of social satire are made to resemble real commercial billboards.
Source: http://www.graffiti.org

RON ENGLISH
Monica Marilyn
New York, 1998
Project: Part of an ongoing "guerilla" billboard campaign beginning in 1982 in which works of social satire are made to resemble real commercial billboards.
Source: http://www.graffiti.org

RON ENGLISH
Hook any new kids
New York, 1997
Project: Part of an ongoing "guerilla" billboard campaign beginning in 1982 in which works of social satire are made to resemble real commercial billboards.
Source: http://www.graffiti.org

RON ENGLISH
Barney vs. Godzilla
Los Angeles, 1998
Project: Part of an ongoing "guerilla" billboard campaign beginning in 1982 in which works of social satire are made to resemble real commercial billboards.
Source: http://www.graffiti.org

BARBARA ESS
Untitled
Pittsburgh, 1988
Project: Exhibition at the Mattress Factory.
Source: Curt Marcus Gallery, New York.

EMILIO FANTIN
Untitled (United Mis-States of Europe)
Suburban Copenhagen, 1992
Project: *Paradise Europe,* an exhibition of
120 billboards of work by 13 artists.
Source: Copenhagen, Biz Art,
Paradise Europe, 1992.

BARBARA ESS
Untitled
Location unknown, 1989
Project: *Art Against AIDS/On the Road*, to benefit
the American Foundation for AIDS Research;
billboards shown in San Francisco, Washington,
DC, and Chicago throughout 1989 and 1990.
Source: Curt Marcus Gallery, New York.

JOHN FEKNER
My Ad Is No Ad
Sunnyside, New York, 1980
Project: Individual billboard project.
Source: The artist.

**EYES AND EARS
FOUNDATION**
(Mark Rennie, President)
over 100 billboards
San Francisco, 1977-90
Project: Eyes and Ears attached a billboard structure to its building
at 9th and Folsom Streets, which was highly visible from a freeway
off-ramp. They put up a new canvas every two to three weeks
that reflected current events.
Source: Janice Steinberg. "When Artists Advertise."
High Performance, no. 43, Fall 1988, pp. 41-45.

MICHAEL FERNANDES
Inhabited by a Spirit,
Worshipped by Savages
Windsor, Ontario, 1991
Project: *In Control,* an exhibition of six
billboards organized by Artcite Gallery.
Source: Windsor, Ontario, Artcite Gallery,
In Control, 1991.

GATHIE FALK
Two Curves Celebrating
Toronto and Vancouver, 1987
Project: *Painting the Town,* an exhibition of artists'
billboards sponsored by Manufacturer's Life Insurance
Company in 9 Canadian cities, 1987.
Source: Toronto, Manufacturer's Life Insurance Company,
Painting the Town, 1987.

FORMENTO-SOSSELLA
SUPPLEMENTO
Suburban Copenhagen, 1992
Project: *Paradise Europe,* an exhibition of 120
billboards by 13 artists.
Source: Copenhagen, Biz Art,
Paradise Europe, 1992.

BARBARA GALLAGHER
Dancin' in the Streets
Montgomery, Alabama, 1994
Project: *Alabama Artists Outdoor,* sponsored by the Alabama State
Council on the Arts to promote the work of Alabama artists.
Source: Kathy Holland. "Taking Art to the Streets:
The Alabama Artists Outdoor Project." *Alabama Arts.* Montgomery:
Alabama State Council on the Arts, Spring 1994, pp. 13-15.

JOCHEN GERZ
Immobility
Montréal, 1989
Project: Individual billboard projects
in many cities worldwide.
Source: The artist.

JOCHEN GERZ
It Is No Mystery
Chambéry, France, 1982
Project: Individual billboard projects in
many cities worldwide.
Source: The artist.

JOCHEN GERZ
Der Grazer Anschluss- Heute ist Gestern
Graz, 1989
Project: Individual billboard projects
in many cities worldwide.
Source: The artist.

JOCHEN GERZ
Those Who Know Will Say Least
Banff, Alberta, 1984
Project: *5 Billboards for Banff,*
sponsored by the Banff Centre.
Source: Walter Phillips Gallery, The Banff
Centre for the production, presentation &
exhibition of contemporary art.

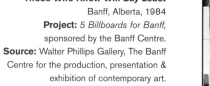

JOCHEN GERZ
The New Derision 1
Montréal, 1989
Project: Individual billboard projects
in many cities worldwide.
Source: The artist.

JOCHEN GERZ
The Golden Section
Essen, 1987
Project: Individual billboard projects
in many cities worldwide.
Source: The artist.

JOCHEN GERZ
Free Stalin Free Coca-Cola
Lodz, 1990
Project: Individual billboard projects
in many cities worldwide.
Source: The artist.

JOCHEN GERZ
Free
Bremen, 1992
Project: Individual billboard projects
in many cities worldwide.
Source: The artist.

JOCHEN GERZ
Les Témoins
Cahors, 1998
Project: Individual billboard projects
in many cities worldwide.
Source: The artist.

JOCHEN GERZ
How Can You Live
Paris, 1992
Project: Individual billboard projects
in many cities worldwide.
Source: The artist.

JAN GILBERT
The Subject Is War
New Orleans, 1991
Project: A series of 8 bus shelter billboards
installed during the Persian Gulf War that led to
another series, *The Subject is Censored.*
Source: The artist.

Survey

JOCHEN GERZ
People Speak
Munich and Brussels, 1993
Project: Individual billboard projects
in many cities worldwide.
Source: The artist.

KAREN GIUSTI
The Green White House
Hartford, Connecticut, 1995
Project: Individual billboard, sponsored by
Real Art Ways.
Source: *The Hartford Advocate,*
August 10, 1995.

JOCHEN GERZ
The Entry
Düsseldorf, 1993
Project: Individual billboard projects
in many cities worldwide.
Source: The artist.

FELIX GONZALEZ-TORRES
Untitled (People with AIDS)
New York, 1989
Project: Commemorates the 20th anniversary of the
Stonewall Rebellion, commissioned by
the Public Art Fund, Inc.
Source: Los Angeles, Museum of Contemporary Art,
Felix Gonzalez-Torres, 1994 p. 33.

FELIX GONZALEZ-TORRES
Untitled (Health Care is a Right)
New York, 1990-91
Project: In conjunction with Day Without Art, shown at ten locations, sponsored by Intar Gallery, New York.
Source: New York, Guggenheim Museum, *Felix Gonzalez-Torres,* 1995, p. 164.

FELIX GONZALEZ-TORRES
Untitled (for Jeff)
Stockholm, 1992-93
Project: Displayed in 30 locations in Stockholm in 1992-93 in conjunction with the exhibition *FGT* at Magazin 3.
Source: New York, Guggenheim Museum, *Felix Gonzalez-Torres,* 1995.

FELIX GONZALEZ-TORRES
Untitled (The New Plan)
Kassel, Germany, 1991
Project: In conjunction with exhibition Cady Noland/Felix Gonzalez-Torres at the Museum Fridericianum.
Source: New York, Guggenheim Museum, *Felix Gonzalez-Torres,* 1995, p. 141.

FELIX GONZALEZ-TORRES
Strange Bird
Los Angeles, 1993
Project: Displayed in 20 locations in Los Angeles in 1994 in conjunction with the exhibition *Felix Gonzalez-Torres: Traveling* at the Los Angeles Museum of Contemporary Art; also part of *TRAVEL #1* installation at Galerie Ghislaine Hussenot.
Source: New York, Guggenheim Museum, *Felix Gonzalez-Torres,* 1995, p. 41.

FELIX GONZALEZ-TORRES
Untitled (shadow figure)
Suburban Copenhagen, 1992
Project: *Paradise Europe,* an exhibition of 120 billboards of work by 13 artists.
Source: Copenhagen, Biz Art, *Paradise Europe,* 1992.

FELIX GONZALEZ-TORRES
Untitled (Portrait of Austrian Airlines)
Vienna, 1993-94
Project: Displayed in Vienna at 3,000 locations.
Source: *Die Parkette* #39, p. 62.

FELIX GONZALEZ-TORRES
Untitled (Bed)
New York, 1992
Project: *Projects 34,* 24 billboards of a rumpled bed installed in Manhattan; an elegy to Torres' recently deceased lover, Ross.
Source: New York, Museum of Modern Art, Projects *34 pamphlet,* 1992 (all 24 billboards illustrated).

GRAN FURY
Kissing Doesn't Kill: Greed and Indifference Do
New York, 1988
Project: Bus billboard for *Art Against AIDS/On the Road,* to benefit the American Foundation for AIDS Research; billboards shown in San Francisco, Washington, DC, and Chicago throughout 1989 and 1990.
Source: Musée d'art contemporain de Montréal. *Pour la Suite du Monde.* Montréal: Musée d'art contemporain, 1992, p. 187.

GRAN FURY

*Civil War (When the government turns its back
on its people, is it civil war?)*
Berlin, 1988
Project: Subway billboard; made for
the *Vollbild* exhibition.
Source: Bern, Kulturzentrum Dampfzentale, *Vollbild:
eine Kunst-Ausstellung über Leben und Sterben,* 1990.

GRAN FURY

Just Do It
New York, 1991
Project: Five billboards for the Day Without Art.
Source: Musée d'art contemporain de Montréal.
Pour la Suite du Monde. Montréal: Musée d'art
contemporain, 1992, p. 187.

GRAN FURY

*Welcome to America: the only industrialized
nation besides South Africa without National
HealthCare*
New York, 1988
Project: Individual billboard project.
Source: Musée d'art contemporain de Montréal. *Pour la
Suite du Monde.* Montréal: Musée d'art contemporain,
1992, p. 187.

GRAN FURY

Women Don't Get Aids (They Just Die From It)
New York, 1991
Project: Bus billboard for the Los Angeles Museum
of Contemporary Art.
Source: Musée d'art contemporain de Montréal.
Pour la Suite du Monde. Montréal: Musée d'art
contemporain, 1992, p. 187.

Survey

GRAN FURY

AIDS Crisis
New York, 1992
Project: Individual billboard project.
Source: Liz McQuiston. *Graphic Agitation:
Social and Political Graphics Since the Sixties.*
London: Phaidon, 1993, p. 47.

GRAN FURY

The Pope and the Penis
New York, 1990
Project: Individual billboard project.
Source: Musée d'art contemporain de Montréal.
Pour la Suite du Monde. Montréal: Musée d'art
contemporain, 1992, p. 187.

GRAN FURY

Magic Is Not Enough
New York, 1992
Project: Independent billboard project, made in
response to Magic Johnson's announcement that he
has HIV; sponsored by Creative Time.
Source: John Lindell.

ILONA GRANET

The Beginning, Middle, and End of Time
Location unknown, 1989
Project: Individual billboard project.
Source: P.P.O.W. Gallery, New York.

ILONA GRANET
Breeder's Cup
Location unknown, 1989
Project: Individual billboard project.
Source: P.P.O.W. Gallery, New York.

CHICAGO UNION OF THE HOMELESS & GROUP MATERIAL
Untitled (We may not have homes)
Chicago, 1990
Project: *Your Message Here,* organized by Group Material in conjunction with Randolph St. Gallery.
Source: Liz McQuiston. *Graphic Agitation: Social and Political Graphics Since the Sixties.* London: Phaidon, 1993, p. 201.

ILONA GRANET
Welcome Wishful Thinking
Location unknown, 1989
Project: Individual billboard project.
Source: P.P.O.W. Gallery, New York.

MARTINA LOPEZ & GROUP MATERIAL
Untitled (collage of photos)
Chicago, 1990
Project: *Your Message Here,* organized by Group Material in conjunction with Randolph St. Gallery and Chicago Union of Homeless.
Source: Group Material and Randolph St. Gallery.

GRENNEN & SPERANDIO
We Got It!
Chicago, 1993
Project: Chicago Culture in Action.
Source: Peggy Diggs.

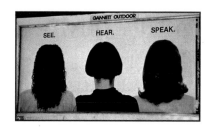

MARY PATTEN, ACT UP CHICAGO & GROUP MATERIAL
Untitled (Talk about it)
Chicago, 1990
Project: *Your Message Here,* organized by Group Material in conjunction with Randolph St. Gallery and Chicago Union of Homeless.
Source: Group Material and Randolph St. Gallery.

JOHN SCHNEIDER & GROUP MATERIAL
Untitled (Hello my name is)
Chicago, 1990
Project: *Your Message Here,* organized by Group Material in conjunction with Randolph St. Gallery.
Source: Group Material and Randolph St. Gallery.

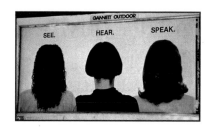

JEANNE DUNNING & GROUP MATERIAL
Untitled (See Hear Speak)
Chicago, 1990
Project: *Your Message Here,* organized by Group Material in conjunction with Randolph St. Gallery
Source: Group Material and Randolph St. Gallery.

JAMES LIEBNER, CATHOLIC PARISHONERS OF PILSNER & GROUP MATERIAL
Untitled (Ningún Humanao Es Ilegal)
Chicago, 1990
Project: *Your Message Here,* organized by Group Material in conjunction with Randolph St. Gallery.
Source: Group Material and Randolph St. Gallery.

SISTER SERPENTS & GROUP MATERIAL
Untitled (This will not be our birth control)
Chicago, 1990
Project: *Your Message Here,* organized by Group Material in conjunction with Randolph St. Gallery and Chicago Union of Homeless.
Source: Group Material and Randolph St. Gallery.

ARTISTS AGAINST HOMELESSNESS & GROUP MATERIAL
Untitled (Why are there homeless people)
Chicago, 1990
Project: *Your Message Here,* organized by Group Material in conjunction with Randolph St. Gallery.
Source: Group Material and Randolph St. Gallery.

STEPHEN LAPTHINSOPHON & GROUP MATERIAL
Untitled (Free)
Chicago, 1990
Project: *Your Message Here,* organized by Group Material in conjunction with Randolph St. Gallery.
Source: Group Material and Randolph St. Gallery.

Survey

ACT UP CHICAGO & GROUP MATERIAL
Untitled (Come Out Come Out)
Chicago, 1990
Project: *Your Message Here,* organized by Group Material in conjunction with Randolph St. Gallery.
Source: Group Material and Randolph St. Gallery.

GROUP MATERIAL
Untitled (When I Die)
Chicago, 1990
Project: *Your Message Here,* organized by Group Material in conjunction with Randolph St. Gallery.
Source: Group Material and Randolph St. Gallery.

VITO GRECO & GROUP MATERIAL
Untitled (My boys didn't die for me)
Chicago, 1990
Project: *Your Message Here,* organized by Group Material in conjunction with Randolph St. Gallery
Source: Group Material and Randolph St. Gallery.

VITO GRECO & GROUP MATERIAL
Untitled (The War on Drugs)
Chicago, 1990
Project: *Your Message Here,* organized by Group Material in conjunction with Randolph St. Gallery.
Source: Group Material and Randolph St. Gallery.

GROUP MATERIAL
Untitled (Are You Locked Out)
Chicago, 1990
Project: *Your Message Here,* organized by Group
Material in conjunction with Randolph St. Gallery.
Source: Group Material and Randolph St. Gallery.

GUERRILLA GIRLS
*Do Women have to be Naked
to Get into the Met. Museum?*
Not produced as a billboard, late 1980s
Project: Commissioned by Public Art Fund, then rejected;
artists wanted to put it on New York buses, Transit
Authority rejected it; never produced as a billboard.
Source: Liz McQuiston. *Graphic Agitation: Social and
Political Graphics Since the Sixties.*
London: Phaidon, 1993, p. 169.

GROUP MATERIAL
Untitled (MLK Jr.)
Chicago, 1990
Project: *Your Message Here,* organized by Group
Material in conjunction with Randolph St. Gallery.
Source: Group Material and Randolph St. Gallery.

GUERRILLA GIRLS
*First They Want to Take Away a Woman's Right to
Choose, Now They are Censoring Art*
New York, late 1980s
Project: 2nd submission to the Public Art Fund; accepted.
Source: Guerilla Girls. *Confessions of the Guerilla Girls.*
With an essay by Whitney Chadwick. New York: Harper
Perennial, 1995, pp. 74-75.

**GROUP MATERIAL and
JOHN LINDELL**
All People with AIDS are Innocent
Chicago, 1990
Project: *Art Against AIDS/On the Road,* to benefit the
American Foundation for AIDS Research; bus posters shown in
San Francisco, Washington, DC, and Chicago throughout 1989 and 1990.
Source: The artists.

FEDERICO GUZMÁN
*Casualidades de la Arqueología
(Casualties of Archeology)*
Suburban Copenhagen, 1992
Project: Paradise Europe, an exhibition of 120
billboards of work by 13 artists.
Source: Copenhagen, Biz Art,
Paradise Europe, 1992.

GROUP MATERIAL
Insurance and AIDS
Hartford, Connecticut, 1990
Project: Bus poster sponsored by
Real Art Wave, a Hartford-based public art group.
Source: The artists.

KARL FREDERICK HAENDEL
Untitled (sign project #3- Quantity and Value)
Providence, Rhode Island, 1998
Project: Independent billboard project which included
five sites in inner-city Providence.
Source: The artist.

KARL FREDERICK HAENDEL
Untitled (sign project #3- Multiple Symbols:
Good Bad)
Providence, Rhode Island, 1998
Project: Independent billboard project which
included five sites in inner-city Providence.
Source: The artist.

KARL FREDERICK HAENDEL
Desires (Love)
Providence, Rhode Island, 1998
Project: Independent project in the
Kennedy Bus Station in Providence.
Source: The artist.

KARL FREDERICK HAENDEL
Untitled (sign project #3- Money Symbols)
Providence, Rhode Island, 1998
Project: Independent billboard project which
included five sites in inner-city Providence.
Source: The artist.

KARL FREDERICK HAENDEL
Desires (Power)
Providence, Rhode Island, 1998
Project: Independent project in the
Kennedy Bus Station in Providence.
Source: The artist.

Survey

KARL FREDERICK HAENDEL
Untitled (sign project #3- Simple Symbols)
Providence, Rhode Island, 1998
Project: Independent billboard project which
included five sites in inner-city Providence.
Source: The artist.

KARL FREDERICK HAENDEL
Desires (Food)
Providence, Rhode Island, 1998
Project: Independent project in the
Kennedy Bus Station in Providence.
Source: The artist.

KARL FREDERICK HAENDEL
Untitled (sign project #3- The Object is
Shown in the Form Most Easily Identified)
Providence, Rhode Island, 1998
Project: Independent billboard project which
included five sites in inner-city Providence.
Source: The artist.

KARL FREDERICK HAENDEL
Desires (Vacation)
Providence, Rhode Island, 1998
Project: Independent project in the
Kennedy Bus Station in Providence.
Source: The artist.

KARL FREDERICK HAENDEL
Desires (Tree)
Providence, Rhode Island, 1998
Project: Independent project in the
Kennedy Bus Station in Providence.
Source: The Artist.

KARL FREDERICK HAENDEL
Desires (Rest)
Providence, Rhode Island, 1998
Project: Independent project in the
Kennedy Bus Station in Providence.
Source: The Artist.

KARL FREDERICK HAENDEL
Desires (Green)
Providence, Rhode Island, 1998
Project: Independent project in the
Kennedy Bus Station in Providence.
Source: The Artist.

KARL FREDERICK HAENDEL
Desires (Heaven)
Providence, Rhode Island, 1998
Project: Independent project in the
Kennedy Bus Station in Providence.
Source: The Artist.

KARL FREDERICK HAENDEL
Desires (Heat)
Providence, Rhode Island, 1998
Project: Independent project in the
Kennedy Bus Station in Providence.
Source: The Artist.

**KARL FREDERICK
HAENDEL**
Desires (History)
Providence, Rhode Island, 1998
Project: Independent project in the
Kennedy Bus Station in Providence.
Source: The Artist.

KARL FREDERICK HAENDEL
Desires (Home)
Providence, Rhode Island, 1998
Project: Independent project in the
Kennedy Bus Station in Providence.
Source: The Artist.

DAVID HAMMONS
How ya like me now?
Washington, DC, 1988
Project: Depicting a white Jesse Jackson, this
billboard was quickly torn down by group of
young African-American men.
Source: Institute of Contemporary Art. *David
Hammons: Rousing the Rubble.* New York:
Institute of Contemporary Art; Cambridge, MA:
MIT Press, 1991.

DAVID HAMMONS
Thank you, Sister Rosa Parks
Springfield, Illinois, 1993
Project: *David Hammons: Hometown,* an exhibition
organized by the Illinois State Museum.
Source: Springfield, Illinois, Illinois State Museum,
David Hammons: Hometown, 1994.

JAMELIE HASSAN
Linkage
Saskatoon, Canada, 1993; London, Ontario, 1998
Project: *Post-Colonial Landscape,* an exhibition
organized by Mendel Art Gallery in 1993.
Source: Joyce Whitebear Reed. *The Post-Colonial
Landscape: A Billboard Exhibition.* Mendel Art
Gallery, Saskatoon, Canada, 1995.

KEITH HARING
Pop Shop baby
New York, 1984
Project: Individual billboard project.
Source: Keith Haring Estate.

**HACHIVI EDGAR
HEAP-OF-BIRDS**
Native Hosts
New York parks, 1988
Project: *Native Hosts,* a project of the Public Art Fund.
Source: Lucy R. Lippard. *Mixed Blessings: New Art in
a Multi-Cultural America.* New York: Pantheon Books,
1990, p. 217, fig. 11.

Survey

KEITH HARING
Crack is Wack
New York, 1986
Project: Individual billboard project.
Source: Keith Haring Estate.

**HACHIVI EDGAR
HEAP-OF-BIRDS**
Building Minnesota
Minneapolis, 1990
Project: Sponsored by Walker Art Center.
Source: *Sculpture,* v. 10, no. 4 July/August 1991, p. 24.

JAMELIE HASSAN
Because there was & there wasn't a city of BAGHDAD
Windsor, Ontario, 1991
Project: *In Control,* an exhibition of six billboards organized by
Artcite Gallery.
Source: Windsor, Ontario, Artcite Gallery,
In Control, 1991.

**HACHIVI EDGAR
HEAP-OF-BIRDS**
Indigenous
Columbus, Ohio, 1992
Project: *Will/Power,* an exhibition dealing with the issue o
cultural identity in relation to the Columbian Quincentenary
Source: Columbus, Ohio, Wexner Center for the Arts,
Ohio State University, *Will/Power,* 1992.
(photo: Darnell Lautt)

HACHIVI EDGAR HEAP OF BIRDS
American Leagues
Cleveland, Ohio, 1996
Project: The billboard draws attention to the degrading use of Native American names as sports team mascots, such as the Cleveland Indians.
Source: the artist.

TONY HEPBURN
Untitled
Ferndale, Michigan, 1997
Project: Installed in billboard space at Revolution Gallery in Ferndale, Michigan, in suburban Detroit.
Source: Revolution Gallery.

HACHIVI EDGAR HEAP OF BIRDS
16 Songs
Dallas-Fort Worth, Texas, 1995
Project: One of four billboards in *16 Songs*, stemming from Heap of Birds' participation in the Cheyenne Earth Renewal ceremonies held annually in Oklahoma during the summer solstice.
Source: the artist.

ARTURO HERRERA
Untitled
Ferndale, Michigan, 1997
Project: Installed in billboard space at Revolution Gallery in Ferndale, Michigan, in suburban Detroit.
Source: Revolution Gallery.

HACHIVI EDGAR HEAP OF BIRDS
Reclaimed
Purchase, New York, 1997
Project: Commissioned by the Neuberger Museum of the State University of New York at Purchase for the Public Art Biennial.
Source: the artist.

KAYE WALL HOFFMAN
Untitled (Billboard Design #2)
Mobile, Alabama, 1994
Project: *Alabama Artists Outdoor,* sponsored by the Alabama State Council on the Arts to promote the work of Alabama artists.
Source: Kathy Holland. "Taking Art to the Streets: The Alabama Artists Outdoor Project." *Alabama Arts*. Montgomery: Alabama State Council on the Arts, Spring 1994, pp. 13-15.

LOTHAR HEMPEL
Sweatty
Suburban Copenhagen, 1992
Project: *Paradise Europe,* an exhibition of 120 billboards by 13 artists.
Source: Copenhagen, Biz Art, *Paradise Europe,* 1992.

JENNY HOLZER
Untitled (Outer space is where you discover wonder, where you fight and never hurt earth. If you stop believing this, your mood turns ugly.)
New York, 1984
Project: From the *Survival* series, 1983-85.
Source: David Joselit, et al. *Jenny Holzer*. London: Phaidon, 1998, p. 56.

**JENNY HOLZER with
KEITH HARING**
Three untitled billboards
(Outer space is where you discover wonder, where you fight and
never hurt earth. If you stop believing this your mood turns ugly.)
(More than once I've wakened with tears running down my cheeks.
I have had to think whether I was crying or whether it was involuntary like
drooling.) (It is embarrassing to be caught and killed for stupid reasons.)
Vienna, 1986
Project: *Protect Me From What I Want,* with Keith Haring.
Source: David Joselit, et al. *Jenny Holzer.* London: Phaidon, 1998, p. 150.

JENNY HOLZER
*IN A DREAM YOU SAW A WAY TO SURVIVE
AND YOU WERE FILLED WITH JOY*
Buffalo, New York, 1992
Project: Individual billboard project.
Source: The artist.

Survey

ALFREDO JAAR
Rushes
New York, 1986
Project: Displayed in New York subways, documenting the
South American gold rush and price of gold.
Source: Lucy R. Lippard. *Mixed Blessings: New Art in a
Multi-Cultural America.* New York:
Pantheon Books, 1990, p. 157.

ALFREDO JAAR
Rwanda
Malmo, Sweden, 1994
Project: *Artownaround* exhibition in Malmo, Sweden.
Source: Deborah Wye. *Thinking Print: Books to
Billboards, 1980-95.* New York: Museum of Modern Art,
distributed by Harry Abrams, 1996, pl. 128.

MOLLY PALMER JUSTICE
Great Balls of Fire
Birmingham, Alabama, 1994
Project: *Alabama Artists Outdoor,* sponsored by the
Alabama State Council on the Arts to promote the work
of Alabama artists.
Source: Kathy Holland. "Taking Art to the Streets:
The Alabama Artists Outdoor Project." *Alabama Arts.*
Montgomery: Alabama State Council on the Arts,
Spring 1994, pp. 13-15.

DALE KENNINGTON
Lunch is Not For Food
Dothan, Alabama, 1994
Project: *Alabama Artists Outdoor,* sponsored
by the Alabama State Council on the Arts
to promote the work of Alabama artists.
Source: Kathy Holland. "Taking Art to the Streets:
The Alabama Artists Outdoor Project." *Alabama Arts.*
Montgomery: Alabama State Council on the Arts,
Spring 1994, pp. 13-15.

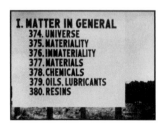

KIDS OF HEIDELBERG
Untitled
Ferndale, Michigan, 1997
Project: Installed in billboard space at Revolution
Gallery in Ferndale, Michigan, in suburban Detroit.
Source: Revolution Gallery.

JOSEPH KOSUTH
Class 4, Matter, I. Matter in General
Albuquerque, New Mexico, 1968
Project: *Portales,* an exhibition at University of New Mexico;
Part of *the 2nd Investigation* now in the Collection of the Van
Abbemuseum, Eindhoven
Source: Harrison. "Against Precedents."
Studio International, v. 178, September 1969, p. 62.

JOSEPH KOSUTH
Text/Context
Edinburgh, 1978
Project: Individual billboard project.
Source: Hirshhorn Museum and Sculpture
Garden. *Content: A Contemporary Focus,
1974-1984.* Washington, DC: Smithsonian
Institution Press, 1984, p. 104, cat. 81.

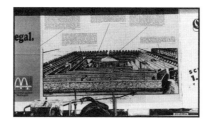

JOSEPH KOSUTH
Agalma's Symposium
Linz, Austria, 1993
Project: Exhibited at the Offenes Kulturhaus, Linz.
Source: the artist.

JOSEPH KOSUTH
Text/Context
New York, 1979
Project: Individual billboard project.
Source: Marvin Heiferman and Lisa Philips, with John
G. Hanhard. *Image World: Art and Media Culture.*
New York: Whitney Museum of American Art,
1989, p. 65.

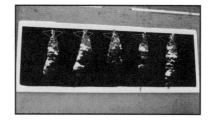

BRIAN KRITZMAN
Untitled
Ferndale, Michigan, 1997
Project: Installed in billboard space at
Revolution Gallery in Ferndale, Michigan,
in suburban Detroit.
Source: Revolution Gallery.

JOSEPH KOSUTH
Class 3, Physics, II. HEAT
Turin, Italy, 1969
Project: Part of *The 2nd Investigation,* in the
collection of the Van Abbemuseum, Eindhoven.
Source: the artist.

BARBARA KRUGER
Untitled
(Surveillance is Your Busy Work)
Minneapolis, 1985
Project: *Artside Out,* an exhibition of
8 photographs by 8 artists on billboards.
Source: Minneapolis, Film in the Cities, First
Banks, *Artside Out,* 1985.

JOSEPH KOSUTH
Untitled
Location, date unknown
Project: Part of the Magritte series.
Source: the artist.

BARBARA KRUGER
Untitled (Surveillance is Their Busy Work)
Minneapolis, 1985
Project: Individual billboard project.
Source: Deborah Wye. *Thinking Print: Books to
Billboards,* 1980-95. New York: Museum of
Modern Art, distributed by Harry Abrams,
1996, p. 21.

BARBARA KRUGER

Untitled (We Don't Need Another Hero)

Berkeley, California, 1986

Project: Individual billboard project.

Source: *Arts Magazine,* v. 61,
#10, summer 1987, p. 20.

SUZANNE LACY

From Reverence to Rape to Respect

location unknown, 1978

Project: This billboard was a backdrop to a
multi-part media event staged by the artist.

Source: The artist.

BARBARA KRUGER

Untitled (We Don't Need Another Hero)

New York, 1988

Project: Individual billboard project.

Source: Los Angeles Museum of Contemporary Art. *A Forest
of Signs: Art in the Crisis of Representation.* Edited by
Catherine Gudis. Los Angeles: Museum of Contemporary Art;
Cambridge, MA: MIT Press, 1989, p. 40.

SEAN LANDERS

Ford 1992 Explorer

Suburban Copenhagen, Denmark, 1992

Project: *Paradise Europe,* an exhibition of 120
billboards split among 13 artists.

Source: Copenhagen, Biz Art,
Paradise Europe, 1992.

Survey

BARBARA KRUGER

Untitled (Fund Health Care Not Warfare)

New York, 1989

Project: *Art Against AIDS/On the Road,* to benefit the
American Foundation for AIDS Research; bus billboards
shown in San Francisco, Washington, DC, and Chicago
throughout 1989 and 1990.

Source: Kristen Engberg. "Marketing The Adjusted Cause."
New Art Examiner, May 1991.

ZOE LEONARD

I Love You

New York, 1994 and 1997

Project: For Paula Cooper Gallery.

Source: Paula Cooper Gallery, New York.

BARBARA KRUGER

GET OUT

San Francisco, 1992

Project: Installed in bus shelters as part of Woman's
Work, sponsored by the Liz Claiborne Foundation.

Source: Y-Core, Chicago.

LES LEVINE

Race

New York, 1983

Project: Part of a 15-billboard campaign;
installed at Ronald Feldman Gallery.

Source: Les Levine. *Public Mind: Les Levine's Media
Sculptures and Mass Ad Campaigns, 1969-90.*
Curated by Dominique Nahas. Syracuse, NY:
Everson Museum of Art.

LES LEVINE
Take
Los Angeles, 1984
Project: Part of a 15-billboard campaign.
Source: Les Levine. *Public Mind: Les Levine's Media Sculptures and Mass Ad Campaigns, 1969-90.* Curated by Dominique Nahas. Syracuse, NY: Everson Museum of Art.

LES LEVINE
Blame God
London, 1986
Project: *Blame God,* which addressed Northern Irish conflict; installed in London, Dublin and Londonderry, Ireland.
Source: Les Levine. *Blame God: Billboard Projects.* London: Institute of Contemporary Art, 1986.

LES LEVINE
Steal
Los Angeles, 1984
Project: Part of a 15-billboard campaign.
Source: Les Levine. *Public Mind: Les Levine's Media Sculptures and Mass Ad Campaigns, 1969-90.* Curated by Dominique Nahas. Syracuse, NY: Everson Museum of Art.

LES LEVINE
Forgive Yourself
Kassel, Germany, 1987
Project: *Forgive Yourself* at Documenta 8.
Source: Les Levine. *Public Mind: Les Levine's Media Sculptures and Mass Ad Campaigns, 1969-90.* Curated by Dominique Nahas. Syracuse, NY: Everson Museum of Art.

LES LEVINE
Forget
Los Angeles, 1984
Project: Part of a 15-billboard campaign.
Source: Les Levine. *Public Mind: Les Levine's Media Sculptures and Mass Ad Campaigns, 1969-90.* Curated by Dominique Nahas. Syracuse, NY: Everson Museum of Art.

LES LEVINE
Create Yourself
Kassel, Germany, 1987
Project: *Forgive Yourself* at Documenta 8.
Source: Les Levine. *Public Mind: Les Levine's Media Sculptures and Mass Ad Campaigns, 1969-90.* Curated by Dominique Nahas. Syracuse, NY: Everson Museum of Art.

LES LEVINE
Attack God
London, 1985
Project: *Blame God,* which addressed Northern Irish conflict; installed in London, Dublin and Londonderry, Ireland.
Source: Les Levine. *Blame God: Billboard Projects.* London: Institute of Contemporary Art, 1986.

LES LEVINE
Master Yourself
Kassel, Germany, 1987
Project: *Forgive Yourself* at Documenta 8.
Source: Les Levine. *Public Mind: Les Levine's Media Sculptures and Mass Ad Campaigns, 1969-90.* Curated by Dominique Nahas. Syracuse, NY: Everson Museum of Art.

LES LEVINE
Hate Yourself
Kassel, Germany, 1988
Project: *Forgive Yourself* at Documenta 8.
Source: Les Levine. *Public Mind: Les Levine's Media Sculptures and Mass Ad Campaigns, 1969-90.* Curated by Dominique Nahas. Syracuse, NY: Everson Museum of Art.

LES LEVINE
Brand New
Frankfurt, 1989
Project: Individual billboard project.
Source: Les Levine. *Public Mind: Les Levine's Media Sculptures and Mass Ad Campaigns, 1969-90.* Curated by Dominique Nahas. Syracuse, NY: Everson Museum of Art.

LES LEVINE
Free Yourself
Kassel, Germany, 1988
Project: *Forgive Yourself* at Documenta 8.
Source: Les Levine. *Public Mind: Les Levine's Media Sculptures and Mass Ad Campaigns, 1969-90.* Curated by Dominique Nahas. Syracuse, NY: Everson Museum of Art.

LES LEVINE
Control Arms
Dortmund, Germany, 1989
Project: Individual billboard project.
Source: Les Levine. *Public Mind: Les Levine's Media Sculptures and Mass Ad Campaigns, 1969-90.* Curated by Dominique Nahas. Syracuse, NY: Everson Museum of Art.

Survey

LES LEVINE
Pray for More
Stuttgart, Germany, 1989
Project: Individual billboard project.
Source: Les Levine. *Public Mind: Les Levine's Media Sculptures and Mass Ad Campaigns, 1969-90.* Curated by Dominique Nahas. Syracuse, NY: Everson Museum of Art.

LES LEVINE
Imitate Touch
Syracuse, New York, 1990
Project: Individual billboard project.
Source: Les Levine. *Public Mind: Les Levine's Media Sculptures and Mass Ad Campaigns, 1969-90.* Curated by Dominique Nahas. Syracuse, NY: Everson Museum of Art.

LES LEVINE
Consume or Perish
Stuttgart, Germany, 1989
Project: Individual billboard project.
Source: Les Levine. *Public Mind: Les Levine's Media Sculptures and Mass Ad Campaigns, 1969-90.* Curated by Dominique Nahas. Syracuse, NY: Everson Museum of Art.

LES LEVINE
Not Guilty
Syracuse, New York, 1990
Project: Individual billboard project.
Source: Les Levine. *Public Mind: Les Levine's Media Sculptures and Mass Ad Campaigns, 1969-90.* Curated by Dominique Nahas. Syracuse, NY: Everson Museum of Art.

LES LEVINE
Green House
Syracuse, New York, 1990
Project: Individual billboard project.
Source: Les Levine. *Public Mind: Les Levine's Media Sculptures and Mass Ad Campaigns, 1969-90.* Curated by Dominique Nahas. Syracuse, NY: Everson Museum of Art.

LES LEVINE
IGNORE LOGIC
Gateshead, United Kingdom, 1996
Project: *Public Pets,* a 5-billboard series displayed on 100 sites throughout Gateshead.
Source: Gateshead, United Kingdom, Gateshead Council for Visual Arts, *Temporary Contemporary,* 1997.

LES LEVINE
PERFORM ACT
Gateshead, United Kingdom, 1996
Project: *Public Pets,* a 5-billboard series displayed on 100 sites throughout Gateshead.
Source: Gateshead, United Kingdom, Gateshead Council for Visual Arts, *Temporary Contemporary,* 1997.

LES LEVINE
SEE IT BE IT
Gateshead, United Kingdom, 1996
Project: *Public Pets,* a 5-billboard series displayed on 100 sites throughout Gateshead.
Source: Gateshead, United Kingdom, Gateshead Council for Visual Arts, *Temporary Contemporary,* 1997.

LES LEVINE
SEE TRUE
Gateshead, United Kingdom, 1996
Project: *Public Pets,* a 5-billboard series displayed on 100 sites throughout Gateshead.
Source: Gateshead, United Kingdom, Gateshead Council for Visual Arts, *Temporary Contemporary,* 1997.

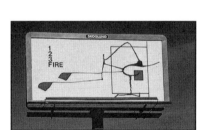

JERRY MADSON
123Fire
Duluth, Minnesota, 1982
Project: *Art in the Air '82*, sponsored by Duluth, Minnesota Art Institute.
Source: The artist.

LES LEVINE
REMEMBER
Gateshead, United Kingdom, 1996
Project: *Public Pets,* a 5-billboard series displayed on 100 sites throughout Gateshead.
Source: Gateshead, United Kingdom, Gateshead Council for Visual Arts, *Temporary Contemporary,* 1997.

GAVIN MALONE
I Will Not Be
Adelaide, Australia, 1994
Project: *Looking at the Billboard* which ran 14 months and included work by 32 artists.
Source: Mark Stephens. "A Possible Interpreting the Billboard." *Broadsheet,* v. 24, no. 1, Autumn 1995, pp. 15-1

ROBERT MAPLETHORPE

Embrace

San Francisco, 1992.

Project: *Art Against AIDS/On the Road,* to benefit the American Foundation for AIDS Research; billboards shown in San Francisco, Washington, DC, and Chicago throughout 1989 and 1990.

Source: Kristen Engberg. "Marketing the Adjusted Cause." *New Art Examiner,* May 1991.

CHRISTOPHER MCNAMARA

The Promise . . . Jam Tomorrow

Windsor, Ontario, 1991

Project: *In Control,* an exhibition of six billboards organized by Artcite Gallery.

Source: Windsor, Ontario, Artcite Gallery, *In Control,* 1991.

FRED MARCHMAN

Be Good! Do Good! Love God!

Mobile, Alabama, 1996

Project: *Alabama Artists Outdoor* sponsored by the Alabama State Council on the Arts to promote the work of Alabama artists, 1996.

Source: Anne Bendheim. "Highway Sports Work of Art." *Mobile Press Register,* Thursday, October 26, 1995.

MIKE MCNEILLY

One L.A.

Los Angeles, 1992

Project: Individual billboard project, in response to the Los Angeles Riots.

Source: Eric La Brecque. "L.A. Aftermath: The Graphic Response to the Riots." *PRINT,* September-October 1993.

Survey

DANIEL MARTINEZ

Don't Bite the Hand That Feeds You

Los Angeles, 1989-91

Project: *Made for L.A.* Contemporary Exhibitions, sponsored by the Patrick Media Group.

Source: Daniel Martinez. *The Things You See When You Don't Have a Gun.* Santa Monica: Smart Art Press, 1996.

SUSAN MEISELAS

Untitled Collage from the series Archives of Abuse

San Francisco, 1992

Project: Installed in bus shelters as part of Woman's Work, sponsored by the Liz Claiborne Foundation.

Source: Y-Core, Ghicago.

DANIEL MARTINEZ

Guerra de Cultura (Culture War)

San Diego, California and Tiajuana, Mexico

Project: *DOS CUIDADES/TWO CITES,* an exhibition sponsored by the San Diego Museum of Contemporary Art.

Source: The artist.

RICHARD MILLMAN

Untitled

Montgomery, Alabama, 1996

Project: *Alabama Artists Outdoor,* sponsored by the Alabama State Council on the Arts to promote the work of Alabama artists, 1996.

Source: The artist.

MARCELO NOVO
Endangered Beauty
Richland and Lexington,
South Carolina, 1998-99
Project: *Street Gallery,* a billboard exhibition
sponsored by the Cultural Council of Richland
and Lexington counties and Lamar Productions.
Source: The artist.

ADRIAN PIPER
Fun
Washington, DC, 1990
Project: *Art Against AIDS/On the Road,* to benefit the
American Foundation for AIDS Research; bus billboards
shown in San Francisco, Washington, DC, and Chicago
throughout 1989 and 1990.
Source: Kristen Engberg. "Marketing the Adjusted Cause."
New Art Examiner, May 1991.

KATHERINE OWEN-POTTS
Northwest Alabama
Sheffield, Alabama, 1994
Project: *Alabama Artists Outdoor,* sponsored
by the Alabama State Council on the Arts to
promote the work of Alabama artists, 1994.
Source: The artist.

ADRIAN PIPER
Think About It
Minnesota, 1983-86
Project: Commissioned by the Minnesota College
of Art for the 20th anniversary of the March on
Washington (censored in 1983).
Source: Del Principe Gallery, Brooklyn, New York.

GUILLERMO PANEQUE
Invisible Symmetry
Suburban Copenhagen, 1992
Project: *Paradise Europe,* an exhibition of 120
billboards of work by 13 artists.
Source: Copenhagen, Biz Art,
Paradise Europe, 1992.

**MICHELANGELO
PISTOLETTO**
Anno Bianco (White Year)
Milan, 1989
Project: Individual billboard project.
Source: Galleria Persano, Milan.

LARS BENT PETERSEN
Notes from the Library (Diary)
Suburban Copenhagen, 1992
Project: *Paradise Europe,* an exhibition of 120
billboards by 13 artists.
Source: Copenhagen, Biz Art,
Paradise Europe, 1992.

KAY ROSEN
Big Talk
Chicago, 1985 and 1990
Project: (1990) *Your Message Here,* organized
by Group Material in conjunction with Randolph
St. Gallery.
Source: The artist.

KAY ROSEN
Hi
Lewisburg, Pennsylvania, 1997
Project: Sponsored by Bucknell Gallery,
Bucknell University.
Source: Katheryn Hixson. *New Art Examiner,*
November 1998, cover and pp. 39-43.

ERIKA ROTHENBERG
Teenagers don't die of AIDS
San Francisco, 1989
Project: *Art Against AIDS/On the Road,* to benefit
the American Foundation for AIDS Research; bus
billboards shown in San Francisco, Washington,
DC, and Chicago throughout 1989 and 1990.
Source: Art Against AIDS Catalog

KAY ROSEN
Untitled
Location unknown, 1990
Project: *Art Against AIDS/On the Road,* to benefit the American
Foundation for AIDS Research; bus billboards shown in San Francisco,
Washington, DC, and Chicago throughout 1989 and 1990.
Source: Kristen Engberg. "Marketing the Adjusted Cause."
New Art Examiner, May 1991.

ERIKA ROTHENBERG
There are Still Traditional Families
Los Angeles, Hartford, and Philadelphia, 1992
Project: Commissioned for *the Los Angeles Festival,*
a multi-media festival that featured three billboards.
Source: Andy Avalos. "They Get Message Across in a
Big Way." *Los Angeles Times.* August 11, 1990.

Survey

RACHEL ROSENTHAL
Honor Our Ancestors: Rats,
the First Mammals
Albuquerque, New Mexico, 1986
Project: *Art/Media,* a six-week multi-media project organized by
Anne Zimmerman and Eve Laramee.
Source: Janice Steinberg.
"When Artists Advertise." *High Performance,* #43, Fall 1988.

EDWARD RUSCHA
Hollywood
Unknown
Project: Individual billboard project, in
conjunction with an exhibition.
Source: Sally Henderson. *Billboard Art.*
San Francisco: Chronicle Books, 1980.

MARTHA ROSLER
Myth Today
Minneapolis, 1985
Project: *Artside Out,* an exhibition of
8 photographs by 8 artists on billboards.
Source: Minneapolis, Film in the Cities,
First Banks, *Artside Out,* 1985.

LEE SALOMONE
As Seen on T.V.
Adelaide, Australia, 1995
Project: *Looking at the Billboard,* an exhibition
which ran 14 months and included work by 32 artists.
Source: Mark Stephens. "A Possible Interpreting the
Billboard." *Broadsheet,* v. 24, no. 1,
Autumn 1995, pp. 15-18.

SEYMOUR LIKELY
Seymour Likely Cares
Great Britain, 1990
Project: Installed in the British countryside by the Amsterdam-based collective, Seymour Likely.
Source: Seymour Likely. *Seymour Likely, IT'S A BOOK.* Amsterdam: Arti et Amicitiae, Seymour Likely Foundation, 1993.

ELIZABETH SISCO with Louis Hock, Deborah Small, Carla Kirkwood, Scott Kessler
NHI (No Humans Involved)
San Diego, CA, 1992
Project: Part of police brutality awareness project.
Source: Mark Alice Duran. "Policing Brutality." *Afterimage,* v. 19, no. 9, April 1992.

JIM SHROSBREE
ZZNN
Ferndale, Michigan, 1997 and 1998
Project: Installed in billboard space at Revolution Gallery in Ferndale, Michigan, in suburban Detroit.
Source: Revolution Gallery.

RUDOLF STINGEL
Untitled
New York, NY, 1997
Project: Installation at Paula Cooper Gallery.
Source: Paula Cooper Gallery, New York.

LORNA SIMPSON
The New World Order
Suburban Copenhagen, Denmark, 1992
Project: *Paradise Europe,* an exhibition of 120 billboards of work by 13 artists.
Source: Copenhagen, Biz Art, *Paradise Europe,* 1992.

SANDY STRAUS
How Do You HELP the Homeless
New York, 1988
Project: 5 hand-painted billboards with large scale portraits of Joyce Brown, aka Billy Boggs.
Source: The artist.

ELIZABETH SISCO with LOUIS HOCK, DAVID AVALOS
Welcome to America's Finest Tourist Plantation
San Diego, CA, 1988
Project: A twist on San Diego's "America's Finest City" slogan, this bus poster drew attention to the plight of low-paid Mexican workers when the city hosted the Super Bowl.
Source: Janice Steinberg. "When Artists Advertise." *High Performance,* #43, Fall 1988, p. 45.

SANDY STRAUS
Prejudice, Beat It
New York, 1992
Project: 24 hand-painted billboards depicting the beatings of Rodney King and Reginald Denny.
Source: The artist.

LEESA STREIFLER
Fear
Regina, Canada, 1989-90
Project: *The Regina Billboard Project,* organized by the
University of Regina Visual Arts Department. Billboards
by 8 artists affiliated with the University.
Source: Donald Kuspit. *The Regina Billboard Project.*
Regina: University of Regina, 1990.

TODT
Untitled (man in bed)
New York, 1984
Project: Independent billboard project
from 1983 to 1986.
Source: TODT.

DIANE TANI
Untitled
San Francisco, 1992
Project: Installed in bus shelters as part of
Woman's Work, sponsored by
the Liz Claiborne Foundation.
Source: Y-Core, Chicago.

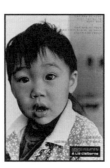

TODT
Untitled (black white difference)
New York, 1984
Project: Independent billboard project
from 1983 to 1986.
Source: TODT.

Survey

TODT
Untitled (man and girl)
New York, 1986
Project: Independent billboard project
from 1983 to 1986.
Source: TODT.

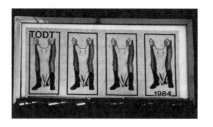

TODT
Untitled (dead pig)
New York, 1983
Project: Independent billboard project
from 1983 to 1986.
Source: TODT.

TODT
Untitled (dark figures, body and flag)
New York, 1986
Project: Independent billboard project
from 1983 to 1986.
Source: TODT.

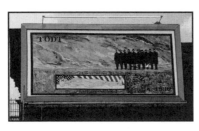

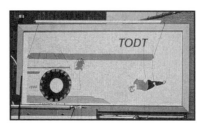

TODT
Untitled (person hanging off truck)
New York, 1983
Project: Independent billboard project
from 1983 to 1986.
Source: TODT.

TODT
Untitled (butcher operating table)
New York, 1985
Project: Independent billboard project
from 1983 to 1986.
Source: TODT.

HELEN VAUGHN
Landscape for a Billboard
Huntsville, Alabama, 1994
Project: *Alabama Artists Outdoor,* sponsored by the
Alabama State Council on the Arts to promote
the work of Alabama artists.
Source: Kathy Holland. "Taking Art to the Streets:
The Alabama Artists Outdoor Project." *Alabama Arts.*
Montgomery: Alabama State Council on the Arts,
Spring 1994, pp. 13-15.

TODT
Untitled (line of figures)
New York, 1986
Project: Independent billboard project
from 1983 to 1986.
Source: TODT.

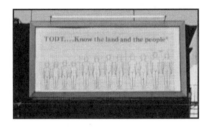

JOHN WAGNON
Quartet Plus One
Montgomery, Alabama, 1994
Project: *Alabama Artists Outdoor,* sponsored by the
Alabama State Council on the Arts to promote
the work of Alabama artists.
Source: Kathy Holland. "Taking Art to the Streets:
The Alabama Artists Outdoor Project." *Alabama Arts.*
Montgomery: Alabama State Council on the Arts,
Spring 1994, pp. 13-15.

TODT
Untitled (flag)
New York, 1986
Project: Independent billboard project
from 1983 to 1986.
Source: TODT.

CARRIE MAE WEEMS
Untitled
San Francisco, 1992
Project: Installed in bus shelters as part of
Woman's Work, sponsored by
the Liz Claiborne Foundation.
Source: Y-Core, Chicago.

CARL TOTH
Untitled
Ferndale, Michigan, 1997
Project: Installed in billboard space at
Revolution Gallery in Ferndale, Michigan,
in suburban Detroit.
Source: Revolution Gallery.

CARRIE MAE WEEMS
Untitled
San Francisco, 1992
Project: Installed in bus shelters as part of
Woman's Work, sponsored by
the Liz Claiborne Foundation.
Source: Y-Core, Chicago.

WILLIAM WEGMAN
The Wegman Brothers
Minneapolis, 1985
Project: *Artside Out,* an exhibition of
8 photographs by 8 artists on billboards.
Source: Minneapolis, Film in the Cities, First Banks,
Artside Out, 1985.

BARNABACE WETTON
Sun Chariot
Islington, London, 1990
Project: Individual billboard project.
In this image the billboard is partially covered
along its bottom edge with small posters.
Source: The artist.

WILLIAM WEGMAN
What Goes Up Must Come Down
Minneapolis, 1970
Project: *9 Artists/9 Spaces,* an exhibition of
outdoor projects mounted by
the Minnesota State Arts Council.
Source: *Walker Art Center Members Publication,*
v. 1, n. 3, Spring-Summer, 1993.

BARNABACE WETTON
Flight to Australia
London, 1991
Project: Individual billboard project.
Source: The artist.

Survey

BARNABACE WETTON
Cafe, Cage
Shoreditch, London, 1986
Project: Joint project with architect Paul Davies
with the quotation, "When you are looking for the
solution to an architectural problem,
remember it may not be a building."
Source: The artist.

BARNABACE WETTON
The Battle and Striding Boots (version two)
Islington, London, 1991
Project: Individual billboard projects.
Source: The artist.

BARNABACE WETTON
Striding Boots
Stoke Newington, London
Project: Individual billboard project.
Source: The artist.

fly!
fly high now,
the storm is coming

BARNABACE WETTON
Fly (fly! fly high now, the storm is coming.)
Islington, London, 1991
Project: Individual billboard project.
Source: The artist.

BARNABACE WETTON
Such
London, 1991
Project: Individual billboard project.
Source: The artist.

LANCE WINN
Billboard for 'SUM'
Ferndale, Michigan, 1997
Project: Installed in billboard space at
Revolution Gallery in Ferndale, Michigan,
in suburban Detroit.
Source: Revolution Gallery.

104

Other Billboard Exhibitions

Survey

21 BILLBOARDS BY 21 ARTISTS

Richmond, Virginia, 1979
Project: Billboards made by local artists were put up at 21 sites for a 3-week period.
Source: No author. "21 Billboards Revisited."
Arts in Virginia, 1980, pp. 8-17.

ACT UP

Denver, Colorado, 1991
Project: *The AIDS Coalition to Unleash Power* placed photo-text portraits of local people living with AIDS on 51 billboards in metropolitan Denver.
Source: Michael Nash. "Street Digital." *Ten.8.,* 1991, v. 2, no. 2, Autumn, pp. 32-39.

ART AGAINST AIDS/ON THE ROAD

San Francisco, 1992.
Project: *Art Against AIDS/On the Road,* to benefit the American Foundation for AIDS Research; billboards shown in San Francisco, Washington, DC, and Chicago throughout 1989 and 1990.
Source: Kristen Engberg. "Marketing the Adjusted Cause." *New Art Examiner,* May 1991.

ARTS FESTIVAL OF ATLANTA

Atlanta, annually
Project: This festival has commissioned many billboards over the years.
Source: *Arts Festival of Atlanta,* 999 Peachtree Street, NE, Suite 140, Atlanta, Georgia 30309-3964

ARTSIDE OUT

Minneapolis, 1985
Project: 8 photographs by John Baldessari, Robert Fichter, David Goldes, Gary Hallman, Barbara Kruger, Martha Rosler, Cindy Sherman, and William Wegman were transformed into painted billboards.
Source: Minneapolis, Film in the Cities, First Banks, *Artside Out,* 1985.
Nancy Roth. "Artside Out" the Inside Story *Afterimage,* v. 13, pt. 3 (Oct. 1985), p. 5.

BRITISH BROADCASTING COMPANY BILLBOARD PROJECT

Great Britain, 1992
Project: BBC commissioned 200 billboards by 15 artists including Michael Landy, Helen Chadwick, Paul Graham, Willie Doherty, Livingston and Lowe, Howard Hodgkin, Richard Long, and Damien Hirst.
Source: David Lee. "BBC Billboard Project." *Art Review,* June 1992.

IN CONTROL

Windsor, Ontario, 1991
Project: *In Control,* an exhibition of six billboards by Christine Burchnall, Carol Conde and Karl Beveridge, Christopher McNamara, Michael Fernandes, Ron Benner, and Jamelie Hassan, organized by Artcite Gallery.
Source: Windsor, Ontario, Artcite Gallery, *In Control,* 1991.

PAINTING THE TOWN

9 Canadian cities, 1987

Project: *Painting the Town,* an exhibition of artists' billboards sponsored by Manufacturer's Life Insurance Company in 9 Canadian cities, 1987.

Source: Toronto, Manufacturer's Life Insurance Company, *Painting the Town,* 1987.

PARADISE EUROPE

Suburban Copenhagen, 1992

Project: An exhibition of 120 billboards, divided among 5 curators (Andrea Rosen Gallery, Galeríia la Máaquina Española, Galleria Paolo Vitolo, Stalke out of Space, Daniel Buchholz), each of whom organized a project with 2 to 4 artists' works on 24 billboards. Artists included were Felix Gonzalez-Torres, Sean Landers, Lorna Simpson, Guillermo Paneque, Federico Guzmán, Lars Bent Petersen, Olafur Eliason, Elmgreen & Olesen, Alan Belcher, and Lothar Hempel.

Source: Copenhagen, Biz Art, *Paradise Europe, 1992.*

POST COLONIAL LANDSCAPE

Saskatoon, Canada, 1993

Project: Post-Colonial Landscape, organized by Mendel Art Gallery in 1993.
Artists: Jamelie Hassan, Grant McConnell, Edward Poitras, and Kay Walkingstick.

Source: Saskatoon, Canada, Mendell Art Gallery, *The Post-Colonial Landscape: A Billboard Exhibition,* 1995.

PROJEKT GADETEGN
(STREET SIGNS PROJECT)

Copenhagen, Denmark, 1991

Project: Organized by the Danish collective BizArt (Louise Cone, Ole Kaag Mølgaard, Lars Lundbye Møller and Jesper Søholm), Projekt Gadetegn featured the work of 112 artists on 117 billboards in the metropolitan area.

Source: Louise Cone. Projekt Gadetegn. Copenhagen: *Biz Art,* 1991.

READING THE WATER

Burlington, Ontario, 1992

Project: Environmental billboard project on billboards in the bay area.

Source: Burlington, The Cultural Center, *Reading the Water: Billboard Project,* 1992.

REGINA BILLBOARD PROJECT

Regina, Canada, 1989-90

Project: The Regina Billboard Project, organized by the University of Regina Visual Arts Department. Billboards by 8 artists affiliated with the University: Jack Anderson, Alan Brandoli, Dennis J. Evans, Antoinette Haerivel, Raymond Ho, Erik Norbraten, Rae Staseon, and Leesa Streifler.

Source: Donald Kuspit. *The Regina Billboard Project.* Regina: University of Regina, 1990.

WATCH THIS SPACE

Sydney, Australia, 1992

Project: Tin Sheds Gallery Billboard Project, funded by the Australia Council; included works by Robyn Caughlan and Boomalli Aboriginal Artists Co-op, Mark Boxshall and John Bleaney, Shannon Peel, Nick Hore, VNS Matrix, Ant Mrav, Paul Westgate, Judith Lodwick, Shelley Cox, and C. Moore Hardy.

Source: Exhibition pamphlet: Tin Sheds Gallery, Sydney, Australia.

COLOPHON

Art Direction/Cover Design : Doug Bartow, MASS MoCA Director of Design
Page Layout/Design : Arjen Noordeman, Cranbook Academy of Art

Printed by **Excelsior Printing Company**   North Adams, Massachusetts
The cover was printed 200 lines on 14 pt Carolina C2S cover with an overall U.V. finish
The text was printed 175 lines on 80# uncoated Finch Fine VHF Bright White Text
Layflat perfect binding by **The Riverside Group**   Rochester, New York

 Made with a Mac